Gino's Kitchen

i16993354

Gino's Kitchen

NOURISHING THE SOUL

GINO DALESANDRO

with a Foreword by Renee Zito,
Executive Director, Hazelden New York

 **HAZELDEN®**

Hazelden
Center City, Minnesota 55012-0176

1-800-328-0094
1-612-257-1331 (FAX)
http://www.hazelden.org

Library of Congress Cataloging-in-Publication data
Dalesandro, Gino, 1958–
    Gino's kitchen : nourishing the soul / Gino Dalesandro.
      p.   cm.
    Includes index.
    ISBN 1-56838-152-2
    1. Cookery.   2. Menus.   3. Substance abuse—Patients—
Rehabilitation.   I. Title.
    TX714.D355   1997
    641.5′631—dc21   97-24053
                                              CIP

00 99 98 97   6 5 4 3 2 1

Color photography by Dennis Becker
Cover and interior photography by Adam Gaynor
Food styling by Nancy J. Johnson
Prop styling by Michele Joy
Illustrations by David Spohn
Cover design by David Spohn
Book design by Will H. Powers
Typesetting by Stanton Publication Services, Inc.
Printed by R.R. Donnelley & Sons Company

Editor's note
Hazelden offers a variety of information on chemical dependency and related areas. Our publications do not necessarily
represent Hazelden's programs, nor do they officially speak
for any Twelve Step organization.

This book is dedicated to our daughter, Hannah Rose, who even in her absence gives us strength and hope. Through her struggle and perseverance, we learned how precious life is. She inspired both of us to live and cherish our love.

Acknowledgments

I WOULD LIKE TO THANK Tom D. White for encouraging me to put my thoughts and recipes on paper. Without his help this book would have remained just an idea.

Dan Odegard and Caryn Pernu for seeing the risen soufflé in the raw milk and eggs, and for having faith in me.

My staff for their support and their efforts in running the kitchen. I know I cannot do it on my own. With their hard work we are able to execute our ideas.

Hazelden for the opportunity to write this book.

The residents of Hazelden New York for whom I prepare these meals. My life has been so enriched by the experience.

My family and my wife's family for their encouragement and support.

My sponsor for passing to me what was passed to him: happiness is the by-product of love and service.

And finally, I thank my wife, Laurie, for her love and inspiration and for putting in so many hours of hard work. In life, as in this book, she is my partner.

Contents

Foreword

THERE IS A VERY STRONG CONNECTION BETWEEN RECOVERY AND FOOD. Most chemically dependent people neglect their health when they are actively using alcohol and other drugs. They come to treatment undernourished and in need of nutritionally sound meals in order to restore themselves physically.

In addition, people who are addicted to alcohol or other drugs become emotionally isolated as they pull away from friends and family. Most alcoholics have only superficial relationships. Addiction separates addicts from the community; sharing meals in recovery helps to break through the isolation of the disease and encourages genuine interaction with others. Recovery is about building healthy relationships, and sharing a meal can help build and strengthen the necessary bonds between people.

That's why, when Hazelden New York opened its doors in October 1992, Gino Dalesandro was chosen as our head chef. Hazelden made a somewhat unusual decision in selecting Gino, an accomplished restaurant chef, rather than an institutional food service to plan menus and run the kitchen. We wanted someone who would embody our philosophy of treatment and show the residents and staff that we do care about them. We wanted high-quality fresh foods prepared with the utmost attention, and Gino's approach, planning menus around the seasons, helped support the more holistic lifestyle that we wanted to encourage. We also felt that since we were a residential treatment program, having a chef would make it more like a family restaurant and contribute to a homelike atmosphere, which would nourish our residents both body and soul.

What makes Gino so special is the intangible but very real contribution he makes to the morale of both staff and residents. He imbues the food he serves with a significance that goes beyond good nutrition. He contributes to a sense of community and shows dignity and respect to the residents in his never-ending quest to create and present superb food. For a population that often enters treatment feeling worthless and filled with self-loathing, the quality of the meals Gino creates gives a very clear message: You are a valuable human being and you are deserving of such quality.

Gino once told me that his job as chef at Hazelden New York is a perfect match for him because it brings together two of the things he loves the most in the world—his recovery and food. The residents and staff of Hazelden New York have been the lucky recipients of his talents. With this book, we can now share Gino with you.

RENEE ZITO, CSW, CAC
Executive Director, Hazelden New York

Introduction

I ALWAYS KNEW I WANTED TO BECOME A CHEF. As a child, I remember my grandmother cooking. There always seemed to be so much excitement in her kitchen. It was the center of life in our family. It seemed as if every important decision was made in the kitchen.

I grew up in an extended Italian-American family—six cousins, two sets of aunts and uncles, my grandmother, mother, and me—all living in the same brownstone and sharing the work. My mother worked and so I often helped my grandmother in the kitchen. She inspired a passion for cooking that lives in me to this day. She taught me that cooking is an experience that requires you to be alive, to use all your senses. You listen for the rattling boil to know if your stock is cooking too fast, smell the fragrance of the herbs as you chop, look to see if your bread is browning properly, feel the vegetables to tell if they are done, and, above all, taste to test the seasoning. Cooking can be therapeutic in that way; you don't hold back, you put all of yourself into your meal. I can still remember the first chore she gave me: cleaning string beans. My grandmother performed even the simplest of tasks with great care. When she demonstrated how to clean the string beans, she would tell me not to cut off too much of the end because that would be wasteful. I took that respect for food with me the rest of my life.

Two of the most basic needs we have are human contact and food. We need one another to nourish our spiritual selves and we need food to nourish our bodies. These two ingredients also play a vital role in recovery from chemical dependency, which is a physical, emotional, and spiritual disease.

Food and recovery are my two greatest loves (besides my wife!) for which I am truly grateful. As head chef at Hazelden New York, I have the opportunity to share the expertise I acquired at the Culinary Institute of America and the traditions of my grandmother's cooking with people who need and appreciate it. Helping men and women who are new in recovery form healthy relationships with food and with each other is very rewarding.

The fruits of life and the spices of one another's company truly make a gumbo filled with flavor! Through the kitchen and dining experience you can see a change of character. Spirit is awakened and there is a new joy of life.

How to Use This Cookbook

A cookbook is a collection of recipes, filled with information to help you in preparing food. I look to cookbooks for ideas, for inspiration that stimulates my heart and mind. I can connect with the people who have written the cookbook and see their vision, which helps to clarify mine. I hope you'll use this cookbook in that way.

I use recipes as a guide, a plan that gives me an idea on how to accomplish what I am trying to create. In most recipes I've tried, I've had to stray from the "map" from time to time, breaking out my compass and finding my own way. A pinch of something else here, an extra minute there, a whip instead of a stir are all things I do instinctively. Recipes can have the same ingredients, but a slight variation in the method of preparation can change the complexion of a dish. What makes cooking so special is the personal touch we add to the recipes. The dishes we cook become a reflection of our individuality and personal preferences.

Whenever I try to follow a recipe exactly, I always have difficulty because cooking is not an exact science. Oven temperatures may be inconsistent in an older stove, or a humid afternoon can dampen your flour so your dough requires less liquid. The best thing to do is just follow the guide, the recipe, until you hit a bump and then adjust. Don't be afraid to take risks.

This cookbook is arranged by season, because at Hazelden New York, what I buy and serve is largely determined by what is fresh and available at the local market. It is an economical and healthful way to eat not only because fresh ingredients are the most nutritious, but also because it puts you in touch with the cycles of the earth and becomes a part of a more holistic lifestyle. Each section begins with a discussion of the seasonal produce and then focuses on one or two basic types of dishes (such as salads, pizzas, breads, soups) that you can add to your repertoire. Suggestions for holiday menus are also included in each section.

As you look through the recipes, you'll see that a few flavorings appear again and again. These are staples that I like to have readily available in my pantry: fresh garlic, virgin olive oil, fresh lemons for juicing, ginger root, cardamom, a variety of dried chiles, sun-dried tomatoes, Sicilian black olives. Most are familiar ingredients used in the Italian dishes I grew up with; others may be less familiar to a typical American kitchen. Most are now available in well-stocked grocery stores, but if you have trouble locating them there, try a co-op or health foods store. I try to purchase herbs, spices, and grains at co-ops in any case because the bulk ingredients sold there tend to be fresher and less expensive than the prepackaged versions available in grocery stores.

Entertaining without Alcohol

Like many people in recovery, when I first got clean and sober, I thought I would have no social life, that life would be boring. But I found I was wrong. Being surrounded by family and friends brings great joy and satisfaction. I love the warm, wholesome environment and feel connected with the people I care about. That is the essential difference in entertaining in recovery: the focus is on the company rather than on the externals.

When I was using, I always felt alone at gatherings. I was looking in from the outside. No matter how beautiful the food, I always felt a profound emptiness between me and my guests. But now, when my wife, Laurie, and I entertain, we get a sense of excitement from sharing the treats we have prepared. The companionship is genuine and the laughter is from the gut.

Celebrating holidays connects us with our community. Here we appreciate the simple joys nature provides while sharing the experience with others around the table, as people have been doing for centuries. It is not the magnificence of the food or the focus on alcohol or other drugs that makes a gathering vibrant and successful, but the shared humanity. A toast is just as festive made with sparkling cider as with the finest champagne—it's the heartfelt emotions and the company that makes it special.

So much of life nowadays separates us from one another. Keeping in touch with the people I love is a priority for me. So when we get together, I make every effort to treat the gathering in a special manner. I want to provide an environment that will nurture both physically and spiritually. I try to provide wholesome foods that will excite my guests and let them know they are cared for. The care shows in the freshness of the ingredients, the joy of the preparation, the attractiveness of the presentation, and the warmth of the companionship.

Sharing a meal in one another's company is an intimate experience that bonds us in a meaningful way. The creative force is the energy between people, and it can be channelled through the kitchen.

Nutrition in Recovery

Proper nutrition is important for everyone, but especially for those in recovery. Alcoholics and addicts tend to focus more on their next drink or drug rather than on their next meal, so good eating habits have to be learned.

Alcoholism or other drug addiction is a chronic illness that affects our lives physically, spiritually, and emotionally. And through food, we can address all three aspects of the disease: Physically, by eating healthier. Spiritually, by sharing the gifts of food with the people around us. Emotionally, by developing relationships with the people we love in a healthy, nurturing setting in the kitchen and around the table. Sharing the gift of food helps us feel connected, one of many and not isolated. Choosing what we eat is one of the most empowering things we can do because it affects us in so many ways. What we eat is strictly our own decision. I believe my quality of life is determined by choice not chance.

After I'd been in recovery for two years, I put on a lot of weight—100 pounds. I was heavy to begin with, but I'd become out of control. I finally realized I needed to take responsibility for my own body. I began going to Overeaters Anonymous and, with the help of a nutritionist, devised a food plan that included three meals

WHILE YOU SHOULD NEVER START a diet plan without consulting a doctor, here's a rough formula for determining your daily caloric requirements:

(1) Take your desired body weight. If you are a woman, multiply that weight by 9. If you are a man, multiply by 10. For example, for a man who wants to weigh 180 pounds: 180 pounds x 10 calories per pound = 1800 calories.

(2) Next, add activity calories: Multiply your desired body weight by 3 if you get no regular exercise, by 5 for moderate exercise, and by 10 for strenuous exercise. For example, if our hypothetical man gets moderate exercise: 180 pounds x 5 calories per pound = 900 calories.

(3) Add the totals from steps 1 and 2 to obtain a rough estimate of your daily caloric requirement to maintain that desired body weight: 1800 calories + 900 calories = 2700 calories per day.

If you want to lose weight, subtract 500 calories a day from this total. This will reduce your intake by 3500 calories a week, which allows you to lose 1 pound of fat a week. This is the recommended amount to lose while maintaining good health.

To gain weight, add 250 calories a day to your total. This will increase your intake by 1750 calories a week, allowing you to gain ½ pound a week, which is the recommended rate at which to gain weight in a healthy manner. Increased calories should come from complex carbohydrates and protein, not from fats or simple carbohydrates.

a day, no snacks, and no sweets. I have lost 150 pounds. I am still no lightweight, but I take it a day at a time. I have kept the weight off for four years.

Becoming abstinent with food, I learned not to use food to stuff my feelings, which has heightened my appreciation of food. When I became abstinent, I experienced a clarity and sense of hope that I had never experienced before. I could finally get close to someone, literally, without the weight getting in the way. As a 400-pound addict, my dating choices were limited, to say the least. But now I've finally met the woman I love and made her my wife. My sponsor told me that as I got healthier, my choices would become healthier. And, boy, was he right! When I told him I was praying for willingness to lose weight, he told me that willingness without action was fantasy. I've come to believe that you don't get what you pray for, you get what you plan for.

So, I planned my diet. I learned that the key was to watch my total caloric intake and portion size. I know a lot of people who constantly watch their fat intake yet still don't lose weight. One of the major problems is that so many of the newer, low-fat snacks are still high in calories. Some people think they can eat large quantities of these snacks without gaining weight, but they're mistaken.

Calories are the measurement of heat energy found in food. Nutritional guidelines recommend that 50 percent of your calories come from complex carbohydrates, 10 percent from simple carbohydrates, 20 percent from proteins, and 20 percent from fats, mostly monounsaturated or polyunsaturated fats.

CARBOHYDRATES

Carbohydrates provide energy to move our muscles, helping us become active and exercise our hearts. Without carbohydrates, the fat we ingest will only partially break down. If you do not take in enough carbohydrates, your body will begin to break down and use proteins to provide energy, which is a very inefficient way of functioning.

Many people think carbohydrates are fattening, but again the key is moderation and not combining them with too much fat. A gram of carbohydrate has 4 calories. In fact, in the United States, we do not get enough carbohydrates. People who eat a Mediterranean diet get 70 percent of their calories from complex carbohydrates and use mainly monounsaturated fat, olive oil. As a rule they live longer then we do with all our technology.

There are two types of carbohydrates: simple and complex. Simple carbohydrates are sugars, such as white sugar, brown sugar, honey, and corn syrup. These sugars contain empty calories. Fruits and vegetables also contain simple sugars, but they are combined with fiber and key nutrients. Only 5 to 10 percent of your caloric intake should come from simple sugars. Simple carbohydrates enter the system quickly, giving us a rush. But they are also used up quickly and we soon crash. Many people in recovery wrestle with white sugar because of its mood-changing characteristics.

Complex carbohydrates include grains (bread, cereal, pasta) and legumes. Complex carbohydrates take longer to break down. They enter the blood system slowly, giving us energy throughout the day. Half of our daily caloric intake should come from complex carbohydrates.

Fiber is a form of complex carbohydrate. It contains no calories nor is it digested, but it performs many important functions. Soluble fiber dissolves in water and is found mostly in fruits and vegetables. Fiber helps lower blood cholesterol and helps regulate the body's use of sugar. Insoluble fiber absorbs water as it travels through the colon and provides bulk. This gives us the feeling of fullness and helps us have regular bowel movements.

PROTEIN

Proteins are essential for life. They are needed for growth and maintenance of all body tissues and are essential for building muscle. The best way to slow the aging process is by building muscle, and for women, building muscle helps increase bone density, which slows osteoporosis. Antibodies, which are composed of proteins, are essential to the immune system. People who are HIV-positive take protein supplements to support the immune system and to build muscle to prevent wasting.

Proteins should provide 20 percent of your daily caloric intake. When a diet is too low in calories, the body will use protein for energy and you will begin to lose muscle mass. This leads to lowered energy and even more loss of muscle. A gram of protein has 4 calories.

Proteins are divided into two categories: complete and incomplete. Of the 22 amino acids that make up a complete protein, 8 are called "essential"; they cannot be produced by the body, so we need to obtain them from the foods we eat. Complete proteins are found in foods such as meats, poultry, fish, eggs, and dairy products. Incomplete proteins (such as those found in nuts, grain, legumes, seeds, and vegetables) lack one or more amino acids. Plant proteins are incomplete proteins, but by combining a variety of incomplete proteins, you can obtain your daily requirements of protein.

Most people need 6 to 8 ounces of protein a day. I feel a 3- to 4-ounce portion size for entrées and 2 ounces for appetizers is sufficient. Amounts in excess of these are metabolized as fats, which leads to high cholesterol levels and heart disease. Also, a high intake of animal protein slows movement of material through the colon, which is believed to increase the risk of colon cancer.

FAT

Many people have the misconception that you have to eliminate fat completely from your diet. This is not sound thinking. Moderation is the key, because fat is essential for good health. It helps maintain body temperature by insulating the body, provides a cushion for the vital organs, and carries fat-soluble vitamins through the body's cells.

One of the reasons people should limit fat intake is that 1 gram of fat has 9 calories, which is more than double the calories in carbohydrates and proteins. All fat is not the same, however. There are two basic kinds: saturated and unsaturated. Saturated fat, which includes animal fat and coconut and palm oils, is the most difficult fat to digest, slowing the circulation, clogging the arteries, and raising blood pressure and cholesterol levels. Unsaturated fats, which come mainly from plant sources, are divided into two groups: polyunsaturated and monounsaturated. The three most widely used oils that are high in monounsaturates are olive oil, canola oil, and peanut oil. Olive oil, a monounsaturated fat, has a character and flavor that are unequaled in cooking. It is also high in HDLs (high density lipoproteins), which clear cholesterol out of the system as they circulate through the bloodstream. Polyunsaturated fats, which include safflower oil and corn oil, are also considered relatively healthy.

I like to combine a small amount of animal protein with legumes, grains, and vegetables, and a minimal amount of fat (in the form of olive oil) to receive my daily nutritional requirements. That is how I try to cook at Hazelden New York, and it is the philosophy behind many of the recipes and menus in this cookbook. It is best to eat a wide variety of foods, keeping meals interesting while providing optimal nutrition.

Spring

Fresh egg pasta and a light cream sauce are a match made in heaven.

Bow Ties with Salmon and Asparagus

Grilled Shrimp with Tarragon Vinaigrette

PASSOVER

Chopped Chicken Liver
Chicken Soup with Matzo Balls
Farfel Kugel
Stewed Fruit

Whitefish Salad with Sliced Red Onions
Brisket of Beef
Honey-glazed Carrots

With spring comes hope. Winter is over and the doldrums are behind us. The mornings are bright, the days warm, and the nights cool. All your senses come to life. To me, spring represents the rejuvenation of the spirit brought on by the change in the weather. One of the things I like best about spring is that there are so many changes in any twenty-four-hour period. The day might go from cloudy and rainy to sunny and warm, with maybe a thunderstorm in between. You never know quite what to expect, although your soul is optimistic for the best.

Spring offers a breath of fresh air, and we feel an urge to let in that sunshine, not only into our homes but also into the patterns of who we are and how we operate. You cannot truly let in that fresh spring air without first cleaning house. Spring is a good time to take an inventory of what we have and what we need and don't need. We look at our assets and liabilities, like in Step Four. When we see where we are and that we are only human, we can let in the beauty of spring that is given to us by our Higher Power. The renewal of spirit gives us the energy to continue.

Among the foods most symbolic of spring and new life are eggs. Eggs are important in many cultural celebrations, as in Easter and Passover, symbolizing fertility and the never-ending cycle of life.

During winter our metabolism slows down and our bodies store fat. Our diets seem geared to keep us warm, with extra calories to help us fight colds and the flu. But with the warmth of spring our metabolism speeds up; we feel rejuvenated and full of energy. As we become more active our diets change, becoming lighter with less fat and fewer calories. With the arrival of the first spring flowers we forget about the barren winter market and enjoy the excitement of the abundance that is to come. The market comes alive with tender greens, sweeter produce, and bright colors.

The Spring Market

One of the most exciting parts of spring is the opening of the farmers market. I find it inspiring to visit the market, talking to the farmers, seeing the varieties of produce in their simplest forms, and getting ideas as I take in my surroundings. I always leave the market with more ideas than when I entered. The growers, old friends who disappeared in the fall, are back in their stalls offering an abundant array of the fresh vegetables our bodies crave.

ASPARAGUS Asparagus comes to the market in early spring. The first asparagus appears as pencil-thin spears; then as time goes on they become meaty and succulent. Asparagus graces the market only during spring, so enjoy it while you can; otherwise you will have to wait another nine months to enjoy this delicacy that has been popular in Europe for more than two thousand years. Usually asparagus is best approached with a delicate hand, letting it highlight itself, keeping it simple. To prepare asparagus, cut off the bottom of the stems, peel the stalks, and plunge them in a large pot of salted boiling water for three minutes. It is best to cook asparagus the day you buy it. If you have to store the asparagus, prepare as above, and then cool immediately in ice water for five to ten seconds, drain, pat dry and wrap in plastic (or place in an airtight container), and refrigerate. You can keep blanched asparagus for up to four days.

BEETS Beets are usually a beautiful red or purple color, although striped and golden varieties are also becoming more available. They sometimes double as a fruit because they are so sweet. When you purchase fresh beets at the market, they should be hard and heavy, not spongy. Choose small beets; if they are too big, they can be woody and tough. When cooked fresh, they are very sweet and slightly crisp, excellent served hot or cold. Beets work well in salads with tender greens and light dressing. Beets are a very frugal vegetable—the leaves can also be cooked and taste like spinach. Beets can be stored in the refrigerator in a covered container for several days.

GREEN SALADS Green salads are increasingly becoming the focal point of a meal. For a successful main-dish salad, you need to use the freshest greens and a wide variety of them. The two main types of greens are those that are mild and soft and those having stronger flavors. The latter types are higher in acidity and more sturdy. When purchasing any greens, make sure the leaves are crisp and not bruised. The head should be tight and the colors bright with the greens looking full of life.

Mesclun is a French term, meaning mixed greens. You can blend many of the following greens together to make a mesclun salad.

Arugula (also called *rocket*) is usually associated with Italian cuisine. The green is peppery and crisp with a distinct flavor and aroma. The leaves should be two to three inches in length. Arugula, with its unique flavor, works well in the most simple ways, letting it speak for itself.

Bibb lettuce forms small tight heads with crisp leaves that hold their shape well. It is full flavored and stands up well in a dressing. Bibb lettuce mixes well with other greens without overwhelming them.

Boston lettuce is very tender, almost buttery, and light green in color. It accompanies other soft lettuces very well.

Dandelion greens are wild greens, mild in flavor with crisp leaves. When purchasing dandelion greens, pick out the bunches with large tender green leaves and no blemishes. Dandelion greens are best sautéed quickly at a high heat and splashed with vinegar to bring out their natural flavors.

Radicchio is a stunningly beautiful green with brilliant ruby-colored leaves. This variety of endive grows in small, compact heads and has a slightly bitter flavor, which offers an interesting contrast to sweet lettuces in a leafy salad.

Red and green leaf lettuces produce large leaves that are tender and mild in flavor. The red and green add color and beauty in a mixed salad. They also work well as a backdrop to an assortment of dishes such as grilled mushrooms or grilled chicken.

Romaine lettuce is mild and crisp and blends well with all the other greens. It is extremely popular in the Mediterranean. You will see it on the table with olive oil and lemon juice, accompanied by bowls of olives, dried sausage, radishes, and scallions so you can make your own salad.

PEAS Peas are one of the treasures of spring. It seems that whatever way we use peas is the right way. Everything they accompany is made better. There are many varieties, such as snow peas, snap peas, and sugar snap peas.

Garden peas are removed from their pods, which are discarded. You must always cook the peas as soon as they are removed from the pods to ensure their freshness.

Snow peas are familiar in Asian cooking, where the peas themselves are actually underdeveloped. The tips are removed and the whole pod is used.

Sugar snap peas are used when the peas are fully developed. They are usually prepared with the pods intact. To prepare snow peas and sugar snap peas, remove the tip and the thick thread running down the center of the back. Then rinse in cold water.

When picking out peas in the market, make sure the pods are crisp and the peas full and round (except for snow peas, where you will rely just on the crispness of the pods). After purchasing peas, use them as soon as possible; otherwise the fiber and sugars begin to break down, causing the peas to lose their crispness and sweet flavor.

RADISHES Radishes have a flavor that is sweet and spicy. Best served raw, they add elegance to the ingredients they are joined with. There are numerous varieties of radishes. We often think of radishes as either small, round, and red or large, long, and white. But many pink, violet, and even black varieties in all sizes and shapes are becoming popular to grow. White radishes are generally hotter than red. Radishes are considered an accent vegetable, rarely served on their own.

When purchasing radishes at the market, look for bunches that are uniform in size with the tops attached. Radishes can be stored in an airtight container in the bottom of the refrigerator for up to one week.

Gino shops for fresh produce for the week at the Union Square farmers market in Manhattan.

SCALLIONS Scallions are a green onion, mild in flavor, with a bright green color and crisp texture. Scallions are frequently used in the salad bowl and in Asian cooking. During the spring, I substitute scallions for onions in many of my preparations to make the dishes seem more seasonal. Scallions are best used immediately because they do not store well. Make sure they are crisp and not at all wilted when purchasing them. They should be a bright green color.

SPRING SALADS

Grilled Chicken with Soy-Ginger Vinaigrette

Grilled Beef with Sliced Oranges and Cilantro Vinaigrette

Grilled Shrimp with Tarragon Vinaigrette

*Grilled Lamb Sausage
    with Warm Potato Salad and Rosemary Vinaigrette*

Asparagus with Honey-Mustard Vinaigrette

*Seared Tuna on a Bed of Red and Green Leaf Lettuce
    with Pineapple Salsa and Wilted Scallions*

TO CLEAN GREENS Fill a large bowl with cold water. Dip the greens into the water and remove, letting the soil sink to the bottom. Repeat this procedure until all the particles are removed. You will know the soil has been rinsed away when the water you are rinsing with has no further traces of grit. Do not let the greens soak because they tend to absorb water. Drain in a colander or dry in a salad spinner. When the lettuce is dry, it is ready to serve. If you want to store it for later use, keep it crispy by wrapping it gently in paper towels and placing it in plastic bags in the crisper of your refrigerator.

MAKING SALADS Greens by themselves are very nutritious and low in calories. In fact, most of the time the majority of calories in a salad come from the dressing. A typical vinaigrette is one part vinegar and three parts oil. That makes for a high-calorie, high-fat dressing, even when you use healthful oils like olive oil. While it is important to cut down on the amount of fat we eat, I do not believe we can or should eliminate all fat from our diets. Fat is essential to the immune system. Fat also helps coat your tongue when you eat, enabling you to pick out and experience different flavors.

I reduce the fat content in my salad dressings by substituting two parts thickened chicken stock (see note) for two parts oil, lowering the fat calories and still maintaining the flavor and body of a vinaigrette. Keep the dressing refrigerated until ready to use.

Always blend the dressing and the greens at the last minute before serving. Do not pour the dressing over the top, but toss it with the greens, making sure it is distributed evenly.

NOTE: *To thicken chicken stock,* bring two cups of stock to a boil and whisk in two tablespoons cornstarch dissolved in two tablespoons cold water. (Make sure the cornstarch is fully dissolved before whisking into stock, leaving no lumps.) The stock will thicken immediately.

Grilled Chicken with Soy-Ginger Vinaigrette

4 servings

SALAD

1 head romaine lettuce
1 head radicchio
1 bunch arugula
1 pound boneless chicken breast (4 breast halves)
  salt and black pepper to taste

DRESSING

3 scallions (white and green parts), thinly sliced
1 garlic clove, minced
1 tablespoon grated fresh ginger (or 1 teaspoon ground ginger)
½ cup cider vinegar
2 tablespoons soy sauce
1 tablespoon honey
1 teaspoon hoisin sauce (see note)
1 tablespoon Asian chili oil (see note)
1½ cups virgin olive oil

GARNISH

1 carrot, peeled and grated
2 scallions (white part only), thinly sliced

Prepare the greens: Remove the outer and bruised leaves of the romaine and radicchio. Tear off the tops of romaine and cut the radicchio in half, removing the core. Remove the stems from the arugula. Wash all the greens as described on page 10. Tear romaine and radicchio leaves into 2-inch pieces and tear arugula leaves in half.

Prepare the dressing: Combine the scallions, garlic, ginger, vinegar, soy sauce, honey, and hoisin sauce in a bowl and let sit 20 minutes. Whisk vigorously with a wire whisk while slowly adding the chili oil and olive oil, making an emulsion.

Cook the chicken: Grill the chicken breast over a grill sprayed with nonstick coating (or sear over high heat in a nonstick pan). Cook on each side about 5 minutes. Sprinkle with salt and pepper to taste. Remove from the grill, cut across the width into 1-inch-wide strips, and toss with ¼ cup of dressing. Set aside.

Assemble the salad: Toss the greens with just enough dressing to coat evenly (about ½ cup). Mound the greens in the center of 4 plates. Arrange strips of chicken around each mound of greens and sprinkle with a garnish of carrots and scallions. Finish by drizzling a little more dressing over each salad.

NOTE: Hoisin sauce and Asian chili oil may be purchased in the Asian section of a well-stocked grocery store or at a specialty store.

Grilled Beef with Sliced Oranges and Cilantro Vinaigrette

4 servings

SALAD
1 head romaine lettuce
1 head Bibb lettuce
1 head Boston lettuce
1 pound boneless sirloin, cubed
2 canned chipotle peppers, chopped
½ teaspoon salt

DRESSING
1 garlic clove, minced
3 scallions (white part only), thinly sliced
½ cup cider vinegar
½ tablespoon grated orange peel
1 tablespoon orange juice (preferably fresh squeezed)
2 tablespoons chopped fresh cilantro
1 teaspoon ground coriander
½ teaspoon salt
½ teaspoon black pepper
1 teaspoon sugar
½ cup virgin olive oil
1 cup thickened chicken stock (see page 10) or 1 cup virgin olive oil

GARNISH
4 oranges
1 bunch radishes, tops removed and thinly sliced

Prepare the greens: Remove the outer leaves and blemished tops of the lettuces and tear into 2-inch pieces. Wash as described on page 10.

Prepare the sirloin: Mix the sirloin, chipotle peppers, and salt and let stand 20 minutes. Sear the sirloin over high heat in a nonstick pan or on a hot grill sprayed with nonstick coating, about 4 minutes on each side.

Prepare the dressing: In a stainless steel bowl, combine the garlic, scallions, vinegar, orange peel, orange juice, cilantro, coriander, salt, pepper, and sugar. Let stand 20 minutes to blend and develop flavors. Then with a wire whisk, slowly alternate adding oil, then stock, a little at a time, making an emulsion.

Assemble the salad: Toss the greens with just enough dressing to coat evenly, about ½ cup. Mound in the center of four plates and place the grilled beef around the salad. You can express your artistic side by placing orange and radish slices in different designs. Try lining the perimeter of the plate with alternating slices, or place two rows of orange slices with radishes layered over them on half the plate. Experiment and you may surprise yourself and impress your guests! But mostly, have fun. Whatever you decide, finish with a drizzle of dressing over the entire salad.

Grilled Shrimp with Tarragon Vinaigrette

4 servings

SALAD

2 heads radicchio

4 bunches arugula

1 pound shrimp, peeled and deveined (see note)

1 teaspoon cayenne pepper

1 teaspoon salt

   juice of ½ lemon

DRESSING

3 scallions (white and green parts), thinly sliced

1 garlic clove, minced

½ cup balsamic vinegar

1 tablespoon honey

   juice of ½ lemon

1 tablespoon Dijon mustard

1 tablespoon chopped fresh tarragon (or 1 teaspoon dried tarragon)
1 teaspoon salt
½ teaspoon black pepper
1½ cups virgin olive oil

GARNISH
1 cup fresh shelled peas
3 scallions (white part only), thinly sliced

Prepare the greens: Remove outer and bruised leaves from the radicchio, tear off the tops, and cut in half. Remove the stems from the arugula. Wash all the greens as described on page 10. Tear the radicchio leaves into 2-inch pieces and tear the arugula leaves in half. Place the greens in a stainless steel bowl and toss with 1 cup of the dressing.

Prepare the shrimp: Combine the shrimp, cayenne pepper, salt, and lemon juice. Let marinate 20 minutes. Sear the shrimp at high heat in a nonstick pan or on a grill sprayed with nonstick coating until they turn opaque (about 3 minutes on each side). Be careful not to overcook.

Prepare the dressing: Combine the scallions, garlic, balsamic vinegar, honey, lemon juice, mustard, tarragon, salt, and pepper in a mixing bowl. Whisk and let stand 20 minutes. Add the olive oil slowly, whisking constantly, making an emulsion.

Assemble the salad: Mound the greens on 4 plates and place the shrimp, tails up, around each mound. Garnish with the peas and scallions, drizzle with dressing, and serve.

NOTE: *To clean shrimp* before you cook, simply pull off the legs at the center of the shrimp, and then pull the shell away. (The shells can be saved for making shrimp stock or shrimp bisque on page 197.) Devein the shrimp by running a small paring knife along the back of each shrimp, making a slit deep enough to expose the vein. Hold under cold running water while you remove the vein. Place on a dry paper towel and pat dry.

Grilled Lamb Sausage with Warm Potato Salad and Rosemary Vinaigrette

4 servings

SALAD

1 head romaine lettuce
1 head Boston lettuce
1 head Bibb lettuce
1 head red leaf lettuce
8 2-ounce links of lamb sausage (1 pound)

DRESSING

3 scallions (white part only), thinly sliced
1 garlic clove, finely chopped
½ cup cider vinegar
1 teaspoon chopped fresh rosemary (or ½ teaspoon dried rosemary)
¼ teaspoon salt
¼ teaspoon black pepper
¼ teaspoon cayenne pepper
½ cup virgin olive oil
1 cup chicken stock thickened with 1 tablespoon cornstarch (see page 10)

POTATO SALAD

10 red new potatoes, cut in half
3 scallions (white part only), thinly sliced
2 tablespoons virgin olive oil
 juice of ½ lemon
½ teaspoon salt
¼ teaspoon black pepper
2 teaspoons chopped fresh parsley

Prepare the greens: Remove outer and bruised leaves from the greens and tear off the tops. Wash as described on page 10. Tear the leaves into 2-inch pieces.

Prepare the sausage: Cook the lamb sausage on a grill sprayed with nonstick coating or sear in a nonstick pan over high heat. Turn the sausages to cook thoroughly on all sides, about 8 minutes.

Prepare the dressing: Combine the scallions, garlic, cider vinegar, rosemary, salt, black pepper, and cayenne pepper in a large bowl and let stand 20 minutes. Beating vigorously with a wire whisk, slowly alternate adding oil and stock, a little at a time, making an emulsion.

Prepare the potatoes: Cook the potatoes in boiling water 10 minutes or until tender but not soft. Drain and let cool to room temperature, about 20 minutes. In a large bowl, combine the potatoes, scallions, olive oil, lemon juice, salt, pepper, and parsley and mix gently, trying not to break up the potatoes.

Assemble the salad: Toss the greens with enough dressing to coat thoroughly, about ½ cup. Place 1 cup of potatoes in the center of each plate. Arrange the greens around the potatoes and place the sausages over the greens. Drizzle dressing on top and serve.

Asparagus with Honey-Mustard Vinaigrette

4 servings

SALAD

- 1 head red leaf lettuce
- 1 head green leaf lettuce
- 40 spears of asparagus, about 1½ pounds

DRESSING

- 3 scallions (white part only), thinly sliced
- 1 garlic clove, minced
- ¼ cup balsamic vinegar
- juice of 1 lemon
- 1 tablespoon honey
- 1 tablespoon Dijon mustard
- 1 teaspoon salt
- ½ teaspoon black pepper
- ¾ cup virgin olive oil

Prepare the greens: Remove the outer leaves of lettuce and any bruised or blemished pieces. Wash as described on page 10. Keep the leaves whole to serve as a bed for the asparagus.

Trim and cook the asparagus 3 minutes in a large pot of rapidly boiling water. Remove from the water and plunge into ice water to cool rapidly. Drain and pat dry.

Prepare the dressing: Combine the scallions, garlic, balsamic vinegar, lemon juice, honey, mustard, salt, and pepper in a bowl and let sit 20 minutes. Then whisk vigorously, adding olive oil in a slow stream, making an emulsion. Let stand 20 minutes (or longer).

Assemble the salad: Toss the greens with enough dressing to coat the leaves (about ¾ cup). Arrange a bed of leaves on each plate. Place the asparagus in a fan shape on top of the leaves. Drizzle with dressing. This simple salad highlights the best of spring.

NOTE: As asparagus cooks, acids within it are released, which discolor it. By cooking it in a large volume of water, the acid is diluted, and by cooking it as quickly as possible, the acid has less time to discolor it.

Seared Tuna on a Bed of Red and Green Leaf Lettuce with Pineapple Salsa and Wilted Scallions

4 servings

SALAD
1 head red leaf lettuce
1 head green leaf lettuce
1 pound tuna, cut into 4-ounce fillets
　juice of ½ lemon
½ teaspoon salt
1 teaspoon virgin olive oil
1 cup vinaigrette dressing

SALSA
1 teaspoon virgin olive oil
3 scallions (white and firm green parts), thinly sliced
1 teaspoon seeded and minced jalapeño peppers (see note)
1 tablespoon grated fresh ginger (or 1 teaspoon ground ginger)

1   cup orange juice, preferably fresh squeezed
1   pineapple, peeled, cored, and diced (about 4 cups)
1   tablespoon chopped fresh mint
1   tablespoon chopped fresh cilantro
¼   teaspoon cumin
¼   teaspoon chili powder
½   teaspoon salt
¼   teaspoon black pepper

GARNISH
2   tablespoons virgin olive oil
4   scallions (white and firm green parts), thinly sliced

Prepare the greens: Remove the outer leaves and any blemished leaves. Tear the leaves in half, and wash as described on page 10.

Combine the tuna, lemon juice, salt, and olive oil. Let marinate while preparing salsa.

Prepare the salsa: In a sauté pan, heat the olive oil over medium heat. Add the scallions, jalapeño peppers, and ginger. Heat until the aroma is released (just 1 to 2 minutes). Add the orange juice and reduce the liquid slightly (3 to 4 minutes). Add the pineapple, herbs, and seasonings. Remove from the heat and toss.

In a nonstick pan, sear the tuna on both sides for 4 to 6 minutes, depending on how well done you prefer your fish.

Prepare the garnish: Heat the olive oil to the smoking point; set aside.

Assemble the salad: Toss the greens with enough vinaigrette dressing to coat evenly. Mound the greens along the bottoms of 4 plates with the salsa in the middle of the plate. Lean the tuna fillet on the salsa. Place sliced scallions on top of the tuna and drizzle with the heated olive oil, wilting the scallions and giving off a refreshing aroma that reminds you spring is in the air.

NOTE: Wear plastic gloves when handling jalapeño peppers so you do not burn your hands. Mexicans refer to seeded peppers as "castrated," but I find the "macho" ones a bit too hot. Suit yourself!

PASTA

Homemade Pasta Dough

Fettuccine
Wilted radicchio, arugula, and spinach in chicken broth
Scallops and almonds in cream sauce
Pasta primavera

Spaghetti
Meatballs and sausage in tomato sauce
White clam sauce

Fusilli
Lamb sausage and fresh peas in chicken broth

Angel Hair
Sour cream sauce with fresh basil and tomatoes
Spinach, peas, and scallions in chicken broth

Bow Ties
Wild mushrooms in cream sauce
Salmon and asparagus

Rigatoni
Tomatoes and olives topped with goat cheese

Ravioli
Homemade ravioli dough
Cheese with roasted tomatoes and garlic sauce
Scallop with white chive butter sauce
Pumpkin with spicy tomato sauce in chicken broth
Carrot with roasted garlic in cilantro sauce

Homemade Pasta Dough

Makes 1 pound

Fresh homemade pasta is something very special. There is no better combination than freshly made egg pasta with a light cream sauce; it is a match made in heaven. The minute you take your first bite of fresh pasta, you immediately notice how tender and flavorful it is.

Making fresh pasta is a craft, but one that can be easily learned. The techniques aren't at all difficult, although the process does take time. I don't do it every time I want pasta, but it's a wonderful way to pass a rainy Saturday afternoon.

One of the reasons I like making fresh pasta is that it shows I have put a lot of myself and my workmanship into the meal. I know exactly what ingredients go into the pasta, and I really like the idea of preparing an entire meal without buying any part of it premade—I can be involved in the process from beginning to end. My friends and family really appreciate the extra effort I've taken to make their meal.

EQUIPMENT

To make homemade pasta, I use the following equipment:

a heavy-duty mixer (for mixing the dough)
a rolling pin
a pastry cutter
a pasta machine

On the pasta machine I use at home, I can make four different kinds of pasta: sheet pasta (for ravioli and lasagna), spaghetti, fettuccine, and angel hair. With these four pastas I can put together an infinite number of delicious meals.

INGREDIENTS

Pasta is made with a special flour called durum wheat flour, or semolina. This flour is harder than other flours. It is less processed and remains in a more natural state. It has a higher percentage of gluten, making it easier to work with because it is firmer and holds its shape well after cooking. All-purpose flour tends to make a mushy pasta.

6 **cups durum wheat flour, or semolina**
   extra durum wheat flour for dusting
7 **large eggs**
4 **egg yolks**
1 **tablespoon salt**

Place all the ingredients in a mixing bowl and begin to mix at low speed with a dough hook. Mix just long enough for the ingredients to combine to form a ball (about 2 minutes). Dust the dough with extra durum flour while mixing so it does not stick to the sides of the bowl. You do not want to overmix, or the dough will be too tough and end up like a rubber band! Place on a floured work surface and knead for 2 minutes by hand.

Divide the dough into 4 equal pieces, wrap with plastic wrap, and refrigerate for 2 hours. When the dough has rested, turn out onto a floured surface and use a rolling pin to roll each piece into a 8 x 4-inch rectangle about ¼ inch thick.

Now begin to put 1 piece at a time through the pasta machine. Start at the widest setting (#1) and put the dough through. Close down the opening between the machine's rollers by one notch and put the dough through the machine again. Continue to put the dough through the machine, reducing one setting at a time until you reach #5. When the dough reaches the desired length, cut it with a dough cutter.

Pick it up in the middle, twirl it into a mound, and place it on a tray with parchment paper, dusted with durum flour. Now you can (1) cook the fresh pasta, (2) leave it to dry uncovered in the refrigerator for a day or two and then wrap and store in your pantry, or (3) wrap tightly and freeze until you are ready to use it. Frozen pasta stores well for up to a month and should be cooked while still frozen.

COOKING THE PASTA

Timing is everything in cooking pasta. To cook a pound of fresh pasta, boil 1 gallon of water with 1 tablespoon salt and 1 tablespoon virgin olive oil. When the water is boiling hard—and make sure the water is boiling before you add the pasta—drop in the pasta and cook for 3 minutes. If you are using frozen fresh pasta, increase the cooking time to 4 minutes. If you are using dry homemade pasta, double the cooking time to 6 minutes. When the pasta is tender to the teeth but still a bit firm, it is cooked correctly. Drain in a colander and toss with sauce.

SAUCING THE PASTA

People often transfer the pasta to a bowl and then place the sauce and accompaniment on top. This is not the best way to serve pasta, however. It is better to toss the pasta and sauce together, thoroughly blending, so the pasta can absorb the flavors and the textures can mix, making each bite a delight!

I usually buy my tube pastas (rigatoni, ziti, penne) and shaped pastas (fusilli and bow ties) dry. Shaped pastas take a little longer to cook, ranging from about 8 minutes for fusilli to 15 minutes for rigatoni and anywhere between. Angel hair, because it is so fine, only takes 2 to 3 minutes.

TYPES OF PASTA

There are so many different varieties and shapes of pasta that it can be difficult to determine what is the best kind for a dish. Here are some general guidelines that I use.

Long pastas: spaghetti, linguine, and angel hair. These are best suited for olive oil and tomato sauces. The best barometer of a well-matched pasta sauce is how well the sauce clings to the long pasta when it's twirled.

Flat pastas: fettuccine, tagliolini, and tagliatelle. These long flat pastas lend themselves to cream-based sauces, which are easily absorbed. When a recipe calls for flat pasta, it is best to use freshly made egg pasta because of its porous texture, allowing it to fully absorb the flavors of its sauce.

Tube and shaped pastas: penne, ziti, rigatoni, bow ties, and fusilli. These are best store bought and dried. Shaped pasta is very chewy and ideal for combining with chunky sauces, such as chunks of chicken with roast peppers, a meat sauce, or a mushroom cream sauce. Because shaped pasta has so much body, it can be successfully blended with meats and vegetables, and it withstands baking, thus becoming a hearty meal.

Fettuccine with Wilted Radicchio, Arugula, and Spinach in Chicken Broth

4 servings

1	tablespoon virgin olive oil
½	onion, sliced
1	teaspoon chopped garlic
1	head radicchio, shredded
4	cups arugula, washed and stemmed
8	cups spinach, washed and stemmed
3	cups chicken stock
1	teaspoon salt
½	teaspoon black pepper
1	tablespoon butter
1	tablespoon chopped fresh sage (or 1 teaspoon dried sage)
1	pound fettuccine, cooked
1	tablespoon freshly grated Parmigiano-Reggiano cheese

Heat the olive oil and sauté the onion and garlic until the mixture begins to caramelize. Add the radicchio, arugula, and spinach and continue cooking until the greens are wilted. Add the stock and continue cooking at medium heat about 8 minutes until the stock is reduced by half. Add salt and pepper and blend in the butter and sage. Toss with fettuccine.

Divide among 4 bowls and garnish with freshly grated Parmigiano-Reggiano cheese.

Fettuccine with Scallops and Almonds in Cream Sauce

4 servings

I love cream sauces, but like most people, I don't like all the fat and calories they usually contain. So what I like to do when I prepare pasta with cream sauce is to substitute chicken or vegetable stock for part of the cream. I use two parts stock to one part cream. This creates a rich sauce that has less fat and fewer calories than a traditional cream sauce, yet it still retains the creamy richness. If I want to further reduce fat and calories, I replace the cream with evaporated skim milk.

- 1 teaspoon virgin olive oil
- 2 shallots, chopped
- 2 garlic cloves, chopped
- 1 pound sea scallops
- 2 cups chicken stock
- 1 cup heavy cream or evaporated skim milk
- 1 teaspoon salt
- ½ teaspoon black pepper
- 1 cup roasted sliced almonds
- 1 pound fettuccine, cooked

Heat the olive oil in a saucepan over medium heat and sauté the shallots and garlic until translucent. Add the scallops to the pan in one layer, making sure they don't touch, and brown 2 minutes on each side. Remove the scallops from the pan and set aside. Add the chicken stock, continue cooking 4 to 6 minutes, and then add the cream, salt, and pepper. Reduce over medium heat until the sauce coats the back of the spoon. Then add the scallops and almonds (reserve a few almonds to sprinkle over the top of the finished dish). Cook another 2 to 3 minutes and toss with fettuccine.

Divide among 4 bowls and garnish with the reserved sliced almonds. The sweet flavors of the scallops and fresh cream blend together and are accented by the almonds.

Pasta Primavera

4 servings

- 2 tablespoons virgin olive oil
- 1 onion, chopped
- 2 garlic cloves, finely chopped
- 1 carrot, peeled, cut in half, and sliced ⅛ inch thin

2 teaspoons salt

1 teaspoon black pepper

1 tablespoon fresh thyme (or 1 teaspoon dried thyme)

½ head cauliflower florets, halved

½ head broccoli florets, halved

1 bunch asparagus (about 1 pound), cut into 1-inch pieces

2 leeks (white part only), cut in half lengthwise and thinly sliced

1 bunch scallions (white and firm green parts), thinly sliced (see note)

1 pound fettuccine, cooked

1 tablespoon grated Pecorino Romano cheese

Heat 1 tablespoon olive oil over medium heat and sauté the onion and garlic until translucent. Add the carrots and sprinkle with a little salt, pepper, and thyme. You want to season the vegetables in stages, letting each ingredient absorb the salt and flavoring, bringing out its identity. When the carrots begin to caramelize, drizzle in 2 tablespoons water, creating steam that will help the carrots cook. Add the cauliflower and continue cooking 3 to 4 minutes at medium heat. Again, drizzle with 2 tablespoons water. Add the broccoli, continue cooking 3 to 4 minutes, and drizzle with 2 tablespoons water. Continue adding small amounts of seasonings as you add each vegetable. Add the asparagus, leeks, and scallions, and continue cooking, adding 2 tablespoons water for steam to finish the cooking.

Toss the pasta with the cooked vegetables, reserving some asparagus tips for garnish. Mound into 4 bowls. Garnish with the asparagus tips. Top with the remaining olive oil, the Pecorino Romano, and a couple turns of the pepper mill.

NOTE: The sweetest part of the scallion is closest to the root. The vegetable grows from the root up so the white part is the youngest and most tender.

Spaghetti with Meatballs and Sausage in Tomato Sauce

4 servings

Growing up, whenever we had spaghetti with meatballs and sausage, I knew it was going to be a good meal. I so looked forward to coming home. The aroma of the sauce filled the house. When I got home, I would always try to sneak a meatball from the pot. My grandmother would only let me look into the pot. If I dared reach for one, she would let me have it with her wooden spoon! She went so far as to actually *count* them because it was not only me, but my six cousins also on the prowl!

MEATBALLS

1 teaspoon virgin olive oil
½ onion, finely chopped
2 garlic cloves, finely chopped
1 pound chopped sirloin
½ teaspoon dried oregano
½ teaspoon dried basil
1 teaspoon salt
½ teaspoon black pepper
3 eggs
1 cup milk
2 cups fresh breadcrumbs (see note)
½ pound hot Italian sausage (4-ounce links)
½ pound sweet Italian sausage (4-ounce links)

Heat the olive oil in a sauté pan and sauté the onion and garlic until translucent. When done, transfer to a mixing bowl with the chopped meat and mix at low speed with a paddle. When the meat is smooth, mix in the seasonings, eggs, and milk. Add the breadcrumbs and mix only enough to blend the ingredients. Using a 3-inch scoop, divide the meat mixture into 3-ounce pieces. Dip your hands in water and roll the meat pieces between your palms to form balls.

In a large ovenproof saucepan, brown the meatballs on all sides and set aside. In the same pan, brown the hot and sweet sausages at high heat on all sides. When they are brown, remove from the pan and place on absorbent paper.

TOMATO SAUCE

1 tablespoon virgin olive oil
1 onion, diced
2 garlic cloves, thinly sliced
2 2-pound cans whole tomatoes, puréed
  (I like to purée my own tomatoes instead of buying canned purée
  because the canned is already cooked, making it too thick to cook with.)
1 bay leaf
1 teaspoon dried basil
1 teaspoon dried oregano
¼ teaspoon dried thyme
1 teaspoon salt
½ teaspoon black pepper
1 pound spaghetti, cooked
1 tablespoon grated Pecorino Romano cheese

Preheat the oven to 350°.

Using the pan from the meatballs, heat the olive oil and sauté the onion and garlic. When they begin to caramelize, add the puréed tomatoes and seasonings. Simmer for 1 hour in the oven. Simmering the sauce in the oven gives it a dry heat that helps sweeten the tomatoes in the sauce.

Remove the sauce from the oven and add the meats. Simmer another 30 minutes in the oven.

When the sauce is finished, cook the spaghetti in a large pot of salted boiling water. If you are using fresh pasta, cook for 4 to 6 minutes. Double the cooking time for dry pasta. When the pasta is done, drain, place in a mixing bowl, and add some of the tomato sauce, about 4 cups. Toss the mixture.

Divide the spaghetti among 4 pasta bowls and garnish each with 2 meatballs and 1 sausage. Top with a little more tomato sauce and sprinkle with Pecorino Romano.

NOTE: I prefer to use fresh breadcrumbs instead of dry because they make the meatballs softer and lighter. To make breadcrumbs, chop fresh white bread in a food processor. Let the crumbs dry uncovered for about 2 hours. This is a good way to use up extra bread.

Spaghetti with White Clam Sauce

4 servings

CLAMS WITH BROTH

3 cups fish stock or chicken stock

4 shallots, finely chopped

2 garlic cloves, thinly sliced

4 sprigs fresh parsley

1 tablespoon fresh chopped tarragon (or 1 teaspoon dried tarragon)

½ cup cider vinegar

  juice of 1 lemon

2 dozen fresh littleneck clams

SAUCE

1 teaspoon virgin olive oil

1 bunch scallions (white and firm green parts), sliced

2 garlic cloves, thinly sliced

3 cups reserved clam broth

1 cup heavy cream

1 tablespoon fresh chopped tarragon (or 1 teaspoon dried tarragon)

½ teaspoon salt

¼ teaspoon black pepper

1 pound spaghetti, cooked

Prepare the clams: Scrub the clams in cold water using a nail brush. Place all the ingredients except the clams in a stockpot and bring to a boil. Add the clams and cover with the lid. Simmer for 12 minutes or until the clams open. Discard any clams that do not open. Remove the clams from the pot and remove 12 clams from their shells. Leave the remaining clams in the shell for a garnish. Strain the broth through a fine-mesh sieve or a cheesecloth and reserve for the sauce.

Prepare the sauce: Heat the olive oil in a sauté pan; sauté two-thirds of the scallions and the garlic until they become translucent. Add the clam broth and cream and simmer, reducing the liquid by half. Add the clams and seasonings; then toss with spaghetti. Place in 4 separate bowls and garnish with 3 clams in the shell and a sprinkle of the remaining fresh scallions.

Fusilli with Lamb Sausage
and Fresh Peas in Chicken Broth

4 servings

> 1 pound spicy lamb sausage in 4-ounce links
> 2 garlic cloves, minced
> 1 teaspoon cider vinegar
> 4 cups chicken stock
> ½ bunch scallions (white and firm green parts), thinly sliced
> ½ pound fresh garden peas, shelled (about 1 cup)
> 1 teaspoon salt
> ½ teaspoon black pepper
> 1 sprig fresh rosemary (or ¼ teaspoon dried rosemary)
> 1 pound fusilli, cooked
> 1 tablespoon freshly grated Parmigiano-Reggiano cheese

In a skillet, brown the sausage on all sides. Remove the sausage and pour off excess fat. Sauté the garlic in the same skillet until translucent. Add the vinegar and stock and simmer, reducing the liquid by half. Return the sausage to the skillet and add half the scallions, the peas, and seasonings. Simmer for another 10 minutes.

Add fusilli and toss together. Divide among 4 bowls, placing a sausage in each bowl. Garnish with a sprinkling of the remaining scallions and Parmigiano-Reggiano.

Angel Hair in Sour Cream Sauce
with Fresh Basil and Tomatoes

4 servings

Angel hair pasta is very fine and cooks quickly. It goes well with broth or light cream sauce. This is one of my signature dishes. It is quite easy to prepare, and quick, provided you remember to sour the cream ahead of time.

To sour the cream, I place two cups heavy cream on the stove overnight with just the pilot light on. If you do not have a stove with a pilot light, place the cream on the burner in the morning at the very lowest setting possible for six to eight hours. It will not be as sour as sour cream, but will turn enough to give a unique, tangy flavor.

2 cups heavy cream, soured (see above note)
2 cups chicken stock
4 tomatoes, peeled and seeded (see page 160 for method)
1 cup shredded fresh basil
1 pound angel hair pasta, cooked
1 tablespoon Pecorino Romano cheese
  salt and pepper to taste

In a medium saucepan, combine the soured cream and stock and simmer, reducing by half. Add the tomatoes and basil at the last minute, saving some basil for the garnish. Season with salt and pepper.

Toss with pasta and serve with a garnish of basil and freshly grated cheese.

Angel Hair with Spinach, Peas, and Scallions in Chicken Broth

4 servings

2 cups chicken stock
1 tablespoon cornstarch dissolved in 1 tablespoon cold water
1 tablespoon virgin olive oil
2 garlic cloves, thinly sliced
4 cups spinach (about 1 pound), stemmed and washed
2 cups fresh sugar snap pea pods (about ½ pound), trimmed
1 bunch scallions (white and firm green parts), thinly sliced
2 sprigs fresh thyme (or ½ teaspoon dried thyme)
1 teaspoon salt
½ teaspoon black pepper
1 pound angel hair pasta, cooked
2 teaspoons soft butter
1 tablespoon freshly grated Pecorino Romano cheese

In a large saucepan, bring the stock to a boil and simmer 10 minutes. Then bring it back to a boil and stir in the cornstarch mixture. Set aside.

In a sauté pan, heat half the olive oil. Add the garlic and sauté over medium heat until translucent. Add the spinach and sauté until wilted. Add the peas, half the scallions, and thyme, and cook for 2 minutes. Add the thickened stock, salt, and pepper, and simmer for another 2 minutes.

Toss with pasta and butter. Place in a pasta bowl and garnish with the remaining scallions and Pecorino Romano and drizzle with the remaining olive oil.

Bow Ties with Wild Mushrooms in Cream Sauce

4 servings

1	cup dried porcini mushrooms
1	cup dried morel mushrooms
1	tablespoon virgin olive oil
1	leek (white part only), sliced in half lengthwise and then sliced at an angle
4	garlic cloves, thinly sliced
1	cup sliced fresh shiitake mushrooms
1	teaspoon salt
½	teaspoon black pepper
1	cup sliced button mushrooms
	juice of ½ lemon
2	sprigs of fresh marjoram (or ½ teaspoon dried marjoram)
1	cup heavy cream
2	cups chicken stock
1	pound bow tie pasta, cooked
1	tablespoon freshly grated Parmigiano-Reggiano cheese

Rehydrate the porcini and morel mushrooms by soaking them in hot water 20 minutes. Rinse, squeeze-dry, and slice.

Heat the olive oil in a sauté pan and sauté the leek and garlic until translucent. Add the fresh shiitake mushrooms and season with a little salt and pepper. Cook

3 to 4 minutes. Add the porcini and morels; season again with the remaining salt and pepper. Simmer another 3 to 4 minutes. Add the button mushrooms and continue cooking 3 to 4 minutes. Add the lemon juice and marjoram and stir. Add the cream and stock; then simmer, reducing the liquid by half.

Add bow ties and toss. Divide among 4 bowls and garnish with Parmigiano-Reggiano.

SHIITAKE mushrooms are umbrella shaped, with a dark brown cap and cream-colored stem. They have a meaty texture with an earthy flavor and a woody aroma.

MOREL mushrooms have a spongy, honeycombed cap and range from tan to dark brown in color. They have a nutty, earthy flavor. Wild morels are available fresh in the spring.

WHITE BUTTON mushrooms are the most common cultivated mushroom. They are white to light tan, moist and firm. Select button mushrooms with caps that fit tight around the stem.

PORCINI mushrooms are also called cèpes. These strong-flavored meaty mushrooms are a treasure. Seldom found fresh in the United States, they are usually purchased dry and softened in hot water before using. Choose porcini that are tan to dark brown in color.

CHANTERELLE mushrooms are trumpet-shaped wild mushrooms that are light orange and have a distinctive nutty flavor. Sautéing diced carrots with chanterelles helps bring out their natural sweetness.

Wash all fresh mushrooms as you would greens. See page 10.

Bow Ties with Salmon and Asparagus

4 servings

This is one of my favorite spring pasta dishes, combining two classic seasonal ingredients—salmon and asparagus—in a very simple and delicious preparation. It's also an economical way to enjoy an expensive fish like salmon because it goes so much further when combined with pasta. Some people prefer their salmon cooked all the way through, but I like mine medium-rare. The flesh is juicier and more flavorful and does not shred and flake when combined with pasta.

2	tablespoons extra virgin olive oil
8	ounces salmon, cut into 1-ounce fillets
4	shallots, chopped finely
4	garlic cloves, thinly sliced
1	teaspoon salt
½	teaspoon black pepper
1	bunch asparagus (about 1 pound)
1	tablespoon chopped fresh dill (or 1 teaspoon dried dill)
1	pound bow tie pasta, cooked
1	tablespoon lemon juice

Heat 1 tablespoon olive oil in a sauté pan and brown the salmon on both sides. When the salmon is still pink on the inside, remove from the pan and set aside. In the same pan, sauté the shallots and garlic until translucent. Season with some of the salt and pepper.

Bring a large pot of water to boil. Add 1 tablespoon salt. Trim asparagus stems; plunge the asparagus into the boiling water and boil 3 minutes. Drain immediately and cut into 2-inch pieces.

Add the asparagus to the shallot mixture and toss. Continue cooking over medium heat 3 to 4 minutes. Add the dill and cooked pasta. Finish seasoning with salt and pepper and toss. Add the salmon and toss gently.

Divide among 4 pasta bowls, placing 2 pieces of salmon in each bowl. Drizzle the lemon juice and remaining olive oil over the top and serve immediately.

Rigatoni with Tomatoes and Olives Topped with Goat Cheese

4 servings

1	teaspoon virgin olive oil
2	shallots, finely diced
1	garlic clove, chopped finely
1	teaspoon salt
½	teaspoon black pepper
1	tablespoon chopped fresh oregano (or 1 teaspoon dried oregano)
1	cup heavy cream or evaporated skim milk
2	cups chicken stock
1	bay leaf
1	tablespoon cornstarch, dissolved in 1 tablespoon cold water
1	onion, diced
½	green pepper, diced
2	tomatoes, diced
1	cup black Kalamata olives, pitted (see page 103)
1	cup green Kalamata olives, pitted (keep olives as whole as possible)
1	pound rigatoni, cooked
4	ounces goat cheese, cut into pieces
1	tablespoon freshly grated Parmigiano-Reggiano cheese

Heat ½ teaspoon olive oil in a saucepan and sauté the shallots and garlic until translucent. Season with a little salt, pepper, and half the oregano. Add the cream, stock, and bay leaf. Reduce by half and thicken with the dissolved cornstarch. When the mixture is thickened, set it aside.

In a skillet with the rest of the olive oil, sauté the onion over medium heat until it begins to caramelize. Add the green pepper and season with the rest of the salt, pepper, and oregano. Cook 4 to 6 minutes. Add the tomatoes and continue cooking another 4 to 6 minutes, not overcooking the vegetables. Add the olives and fold into the sauce. Stir a few times, add pasta, and toss. Divide into pasta bowls and top with pieces of goat cheese and grated cheese.

Homemade Ravioli Dough

Makes about 24 large ravioli, 4 to 6 servings

Whenever I make ravioli, I think of my uncle. He would get up early every Sunday, make his dough, and start his tomato sauce. The aroma from the sauce would fill the house. He would then assemble the ravioli, making sure each little pillow was sealed so that no water leaked into the filling.

After the ravioli were formed he would put them into the refrigerator to rest. We would all go to church, and when we came home he would cook the ravioli. He said they always tasted better rested.

I learned a lot from my uncle. He was able to show the nurturing and creative side of his nature by the care he put into preparing our Sunday meal.

Ravioli is another form of pasta that is wonderful to make from scratch. The preparation is similar to that of other pastas, but there are more eggs and you knead the dough longer to develop the gluten, which gives it the elasticity it needs to maintain its shape during cooking. You can stuff the pasta with any number of fillings you create yourself. I give a few suggestions, but don't be afraid to experiment.

EQUIPMENT

Food scale (to weigh flour)
Heavy-duty mixer (optional)
Rolling pin
Pasta machine
Pastry brush
Ravioli cutter
Pastry cutter

INGREDIENTS

2   pounds, 12-ounces durum wheat flour (about 11 cups)
1   ounce salt (about 1 teaspoon)
8   egg yolks
4   whole eggs
    egg wash: 2 beaten eggs plus ¼ cup water

Place the flour in a large bowl. Make a well in the middle. Beat the yolks, whole eggs, and salt together in a separate bowl, and pour this mixture into the well. Begin to mix with a wooden spoon, or with the hook attachment on your mixer, until a dough ball is formed.

If you are using a mixer, mix at second speed for 5 minutes. If you are mixing by hand, knead the dough on a lightly floured surface for 10 minutes. To knead by hand, use the heel of your palm. Push the dough down and away from yourself; then pull over toward you, folding the dough in half. Press down and rotate the dough sideways, and then repeat. Continue this process for 10 minutes. Keep the work surface dusted with durum flour to prevent the dough from sticking. When the dough has been kneaded and feels smooth, wrap in plastic and let rest for 20 minutes in the refrigerator.

Separate the dough into 4 equal pieces. Roll each piece ½ inch thick with a rolling pin. Send the dough through the pasta machine 3 times, each time closing down the opening between the machine's rollers by one notch. The first setting is at 1, next 3, then 5. Your finished product will be 4 large flat sheets.

FILLING THE RAVIOLI

Dust your work surface with durum flour. On 2 of the sheets, place 1 tablespoon of filling for each ravioli, 1 inch apart in each direction. Brush around each filling with egg wash. Place the remaining 2 sheets of dough on top of the 2 sheets with filling.

With a ravioli cutter, stamp out the ravioli, making sure they are completely sealed. If they are not cut completely through, use a pastry cutter to separate. When finished, place on a floured tray and set in refrigerator to rest.

Ravioli freeze very well. Place on a tray dusted with durum flour and wrap with plastic wrap. They will store in the freezer up to 1 month.

COOKING THE RAVIOLI

Bring a large stockpot of salted water to boil. Cook the ravioli in the boiling water until tender, about 6 minutes (if you are using frozen ravioli, boil about 12 minutes). Make sure that you have a large amount of water so the ravioli can move around in the pot. Use 6 quarts water to 1 pound ravioli. (For this recipe you will need 12 quarts of water. You can use 2 stockpots with 6 quarts of water each.) To test for doneness, take 1 out, cut in half, and test the tenderness of the dough. When cooked to your liking, they are ready to be tossed with sauce and placed in a pasta bowl.

ALTERNATIVES TO HOMEMADE RAVIOLI DOUGH

There are two easy methods of cutting time on making ravioli at home, and both work pretty well with any of these fillings and sauces.

(1) You can buy sheets of pasta from a specialty store so you can stuff the ravioli with the fillings of your choice.

(2) You can use wonton wrappers, which you can find in the refrigerated section of most grocery stores. Wonton wrappers aren't sold in big sheets like ravioli dough, but the basic method for forming the ravioli is the same. Place a tablespoon of filling onto a wrapper, brush around it with egg wash, cover with another wrapper, and cut to shape.

Cheese Ravioli with Roasted Tomatoes and Garlic Sauce

4 to 6 servings

Homemade ravioli dough (see page 35)

FILLING

1 pound ricotta cheese

3 eggs

½ cup Parmigiano-Reggiano cheese

1 cup fresh breadcrumbs

2 teaspoons dried oregano

1 teaspoon salt

½ teaspoon black pepper

SAUCE

10 tomatoes
 1 tablespoon plus 1 teaspoon virgin olive oil
 2 teaspoons salt
 1 head garlic
 1 tablespoon sugar
 2 shallots, finely chopped
 1 tablespoon chopped fresh Italian parsley
 4 sprigs of parsley
 1 tablespoon freshly grated Pecorino Romano cheese

Prepare the filling: Place all ingredients in a bowl and mix thoroughly. Fill the ravioli and refrigerate until the sauce is ready.

Prepare the sauce: Cut the tomatoes in half, rub with 1 teaspoon of the olive oil, sprinkle with 1 teaspoon of the salt, and place in a large baking pan. Place in the oven overnight either with the pilot light on or set on "warm." The next day, peel the tomatoes and squeeze out the seeds. Purée half and dice the other half. Reserve 2 teaspoons of the juices that have collected in the pan.

Rub the head of garlic with the remaining tablespoon of olive oil, 1 teaspoon of salt, and sugar and roast at 350° until tender, about 30 minutes. Remove from the oven and let cool, reserving the olive oil. Remove the pulp from the skin and mash.

Mix together the reserved tomato liquid and 2 teaspoons of the olive oil reserved from the garlic. Use half of this to sauté the shallots until translucent. Add the tomatoes (both puréed and diced) and garlic and simmer 20 minutes. Add the parsley and stir. Drizzle with the remaining 2 teaspoons olive oil mixture.

Assemble the dish: Cook the ravioli in a large pot of salted boiling water. When they are done as you like them, transfer to a bowl and toss with the sauce. Divide among 4 bowls; garnish with a sprig of parsley and grated cheese.

This dish is usually served in late spring, getting you ready for what is to come.

Scallop Ravioli with White Chive Butter Sauce

4 to 6 servings

Homemade ravioli dough (see page 35)

FILLING

1 pound scallops
1 tablespoon chopped chives
pinch salt and pepper

SAUCE

3 shallots, finely chopped
1 pound (4 sticks) butter, softened
½ cup white vinegar
2 cups heavy cream
juice of 1 lemon
1 tablespoon chopped chives
salt and pepper to taste

Prepare the filling: Chop the scallops finely with a French knife by hand. Mix in the chives, salt, and pepper. Refrigerate until ready to use.

Prepare the sauce: Sauté the shallots with 1 tablespoon butter. Add the vinegar, and cook at high heat, letting the liquid reduce to near dry. Add the heavy cream; reduce heat so cream can simmer. Reduce the volume of the sauce by half. Whip in the soft butter. Strain through a fine-mesh sieve. Season with the lemon juice and chives.

Assemble the dish: Cook the ravioli. When they are done, toss in a bowl with the sauce. Place 4 ravioli in each pasta bowl. Sprinkle some chives over the top to decorate, season with salt and pepper, and serve immediately.

Pumpkin Ravioli with
Spicy Tomato Sauce in Chicken Broth

4 to 6 servings

The sweetness of the pumpkin and the smoky heat of the chipotles smoothed over by the butter create an excellent combination of flavors that will blend together in your mouth. You can use canned pumpkin purée to save time—especially since fresh pumpkins can be hard to come by in the spring.

Homemade ravioli dough (see page 35)

FILLING

1 pumpkin (you will need 1 pound or 4 cups uncooked pulp,
  or use one 15-ounce can of pumpkin purée)
2 teaspoons virgin olive oil
½ onion, finely chopped
3 garlic cloves, finely chopped
½ teaspoon cardamom
¼ teaspoon nutmeg
1 teaspoon salt
½ teaspoon black pepper
3 eggs
2 cups fresh breadcrumbs (dry breadcrumbs have a sandpapery texture that
  does not work well)

SAUCE

1 teaspoon virgin olive oil
3 shallots, finely chopped
2 garlic cloves, finely chopped
7 tomatoes, peeled, seeded, and diced (see page 160)
¼ teaspoon chili pepper
¼ teaspoon cumin
1 teaspoon salt
½ teaspoon black pepper
2 tablespoons chipotle peppers
1 cup chicken stock

1 tablespoon cornstarch, dissolved in 1 tablespoon cold water
1 tablespoon soft butter
1 tablespoon freshly grated Parmigiano-Reggiano cheese

Prepare the filling: Cut the pumpkin in half and scoop out the seeds. Rub with 1 teaspoon olive oil, sprinkle with salt, and roast at 400° until tender. Remove the pulp, purée, and set aside.

Heat 1 teaspoon olive oil in a skillet and sauté the onion and garlic until translucent. Add the pumpkin purée and heat thoroughly, simmering 6 to 8 minutes. Remove from the stove and let cool. Add the cardamom, nutmeg, salt, pepper, eggs, and breadcrumbs; blend together and stuff the ravioli.

Prepare the sauce: Heat the olive oil in a sauté pan and sauté the shallots and garlic until translucent. Add the tomatoes and continue cooking for 3 to 4 minutes. Add the chili pepper, cumin, salt, pepper, and chipotle peppers. Simmer for 3 to 4 minutes; then add the stock. Bring to a boil and simmer another 10 minutes. Thicken with cornstarch dissolved in 1 tablespoon cold water. Blend in the butter to smooth the heat of the peppers and to give the sauce a rich taste. Cook the ravioli in a large pot of rapidly boiling water. In a large bowl, toss the cooked ravioli with the sauce. Place in 4 bowls and garnish with Parmigiano-Reggiano.

Carrot Ravioli with Roasted Garlic in Cilantro Sauce

4 to 6 servings

Homemade ravioli dough (see page 35)

FILLING
10 carrots, peeled and thinly sliced
1 tablespoon plus 2 teaspoons virgin olive oil
1 onion, thinly sliced
1 bay leaf
3 or 4 sprigs cilantro
2 teaspoons salt
½ teaspoon black pepper

2 tablespoons sugar

1 head garlic

3 eggs

2 cups fresh breadcrumbs

Place the carrots, 2 teaspoons of the olive oil, onion, bay leaf, cilantro, and 1 teaspoon of the salt in a stockpot with 4 cups water. Bring to a boil and cook until tender. Remove the carrots and onion from the water. Remove the bay leaf from the carrots and then purée. Reserve 2 cups carrot broth to use with the sauce.

Place the garlic, 1 tablespoon of olive oil, 1 tablespoon of sugar, and 1 teaspoon of salt in an ovenproof dish. Roast at 350° until the garlic is tender, about 30 minutes. When the garlic is cool, remove from the skin and mash the pulp. Reserve the olive oil to use in the sauce. Add to the puréed carrots. Then add the eggs and breadcrumbs. Blend together and refrigerate for 1 hour; then use to fill the ravioli.

CHICKEN BROTH WITH CILANTRO SAUCE

1 teaspoon olive oil (reserved from roasted garlic)

2 shallots, finely chopped

2 garlic cloves, finely chopped

½ teaspoon salt

¼ teaspoon black pepper

1 bay leaf

2 tablespoons freshly chopped cilantro

½ cup cider vinegar

juice of ½ lemon

1 cup chicken stock or vegetable stock

2 cups carrot broth

1 tablespoon cornstarch, dissolved in 1 tablespoon water

1 tablespoon freshly grated Parmigiano-Reggiano cheese

In a sauté pan, sauté the shallots and garlic in olive oil. Add the salt, pepper, and bay leaf and half the cilantro. Stir continuously, cooking 3 to 4 minutes. Deglaze with the vinegar and lemon juice. Reduce to near dry; then add the stock and carrot broth and simmer for 20 minutes. Thicken with the cornstarch mixed with 1 tablespoon cold water.

Cook the ravioli in a large pot of rapidly boiling water. Finish the sauce with the rest of the cilantro, toss the cooked ravioli with the sauce, and serve. Garnish with a sprig of cilantro and grated cheese.

PASSOVER MENU

Chopped Chicken Liver

Whitefish Salad with Sliced Red Onions

Chicken Soup with Matzo Balls

Brisket of Beef

Farfel Kugel

Honey-glazed Carrots

Stewed Fruit

THE EXCITEMENT OF PASSOVER with the gathering of family and the sharing of different foods makes it a most enjoyable holiday. In the Jewish tradition, the table is like an altar. The foods of the seder dinner at Passover symbolize events and experiences of the ancient Jews. Matzo—the traditional thin, unleavened bread—is eaten during the holiday, to remind us of the hasty departure of the people of Israel from Egypt.

Passover is the celebration of the escape of the people of Israel from the bondage of the Egyptian pharaoh. The holiday reminds us of the continuing battle for freedom. I think of myself and my freedom from active addiction; it is a daily reprieve, contingent on my spiritual condition.

It is a tradition to clean house thoroughly before Passover—a spring cleaning. Before harvesting the grain of spring, families remove all fermented dough, which symbolizes starting over, starting spring with hope.

Passover is a family holiday, protesting against unrighteousness, and reminding us that wrong will eventually meet with retribution. It's a reminder that taking advantage of others is not right.

When I think of Jewish cooking, I think of the kosher dietary laws. Many religions have dietary codes, mainly to protect people from disease and to keep them healthy; after all, what could be more spiritual than good health.

Chopped Chicken Liver

4 servings

This is a chicken liver spread. It is one of my wife's favorite foods during Passover. Although not to everyone's taste (admittedly, I am one of them!), if I didn't include it, Laurie would feel that it wouldn't really be Passover.

- 1 tablespoon canola oil (the taste of olive oil is too dominant for the taste of the chicken liver)
- 1 onion, thinly sliced
- 1 pound chicken livers
- 4 hard-boiled eggs
- 1 teaspoon salt
- ½ teaspoon black pepper

Heat the oil in a sauté pan and sauté the onion until translucent. Add the chicken livers and cook at medium heat, stirring occasionally, about 6 minutes.

Place in a food processor and process until the livers are coarsely chopped, or chop by hand. When Laurie was growing up, her family would place the livers in a shallow wooden bowl and use a single-blade chopper to chop the livers, then the eggs. Laurie tells me that her grandmother used chicken fat in the recipe (instead of canola oil), very delicious but considered too high in fat these days.

When the livers are almost done, add the hard-boiled eggs and salt and pepper. Make sure you do not process the eggs too much. You should be able to see them in the spread.

Place on the table before you sit down to eat, and serve with matzo crackers.

Whitefish Salad with Sliced Red Onions

4 servings

- 1 head green leaf lettuce
- 1 head red leaf lettuce
- 1 head Bibb lettuce
- 1 pound smoked whitefish

½ onion

2 stalks celery

½ cup mayonnaise

juice of ½ lemon (before you extract the juice, finely grate the yellow outer rind of the lemon and save for the stewed fruit later in menu)

2 teaspoons Dijon mustard

¼ teaspoon black pepper

½ red onion, thinly sliced

3 radishes, freshly grated

Remove the outer and blemished leaves of the lettuces and wash as described on page 10. Refrigerate until ready to use.

Make sure all the bones are removed from the whitefish. Purée the whitefish, onion, and celery separately in the food processor. If you don't have a food processor, chop everything as finely as possible. When puréed, mix together. Add the mayonnaise, lemon juice, pepper, and mustard, and mix with a spoon until well blended.

Place the greens along the bottom of a serving platter and place the fish in the center. Overlap red onion slices on top and garnish with radishes.

Chicken Soup with Matzo Balls

4 servings

Chicken soup with matzo balls in Laurie's home was similar to spaghetti and meatballs in mine. There is an incredibly soothing aroma when chicken soup is cooking, like everything's going to be okay. And watch out for disappearing matzo balls! Chicken soup has been described as Jewish penicillin and I believe it works.

Laurie and I had a slight difference of opinion over the preparation of chicken soup. She does not remove and shred the chicken; you can take your pick!

CHICKEN SOUP

1 whole chicken

2 tablespoons chopped fresh dill (or 2 teaspoons dried dill)

2   tablespoons chopped fresh parsley
1   teaspoon salt
½   teaspoon black pepper
1   bay leaf
2   onions, quartered
3   parsnips, peeled, cut into 4 pieces
4   carrots, peeled, cut into 4 pieces
3   stalks celery, cut into 4 pieces

Place the chicken in a stockpot with the seasonings, cover with water, and bring to a boil. Reduce the heat and simmer 1 hour. Remove the chicken and place in a bowl to cool. Add the vegetables to the broth and simmer another 30 minutes. Remove the skin from the chicken and shred the meat off the bones. Return the chicken meat to the soup and it is ready to serve.

MATZO BALLS

4   eggs
½   cup chicken stock or water
⅓   cup vegetable shortening, melted
1   teaspoon salt
1   tablespoon sliced scallions (optional—not in traditional recipe)
1   cup matzo meal

In a mixing bowl, place the eggs, water, shortening, salt, and scallions and whisk. Stir in the matzo meal until well blended. Let rest 20 minutes in the refrigerator. Resting will make the matzo balls softer. Laurie prefers denser matzo balls and lets them rest only 10 minutes.

In a stockpot, add 1 teaspoon salt to 1 gallon of water and bring to a boil. You can either form round balls with your moistened hands or just drop the batter in with a tablespoon. The reason you cook the matzo balls separately is that they tend to break up, making the soup cloudy. Cook 15 minutes. Remove with a slotted spoon and add to the chicken soup.

THE FOLLOWING THREE RECIPES make up the main course in the Passover menu.

Brisket of Beef

4 servings

BRISKET

2 pounds brisket of beef
1 teaspoon salt
½ teaspoon black pepper
2 onions, sliced
1 tablespoon virgin olive oil
2 quarts chicken stock, preferably homemade
1 bay leaf
4 sprigs fresh thyme (or ½ teaspoon dried thyme)

SAUCE

1 teaspoon virgin olive oil
½ onion, thinly sliced
1 carrot, peeled and thinly sliced
1 stalk leek (white part only), thinly sliced
all cooking liquid from braised beef

GARNISH

1 onion, thinly sliced
2 tablespoons matzo meal
2 tablespoons virgin olive oil

Preheat the oven to 350°.

Prepare the brisket: Trim excess fat from the brisket and rub with salt and pepper. In a brazier, brown the brisket and onions on both sides in olive oil over high heat. When brown, pour in the stock and seasonings, covering two-thirds of the meat. Bring to a boil, place in the oven, and braise for 45 minutes. Turn the meat over and braise another 45 minutes. When the meat is tender, remove from the brazier and place in a pan. Pour 1 cup of cooking liquid over the meat, cover with plastic, and set aside. Strain the remaining cooking liquid through a sieve and save to use in the sauce.

Prepare the sauce: In a saucepan, heat the olive oil; add the onion, carrot, and leek. Stir, cooking over medium heat. Cook until all the vegetables are caramelized. Add the cooking liquid and simmer 1 hour. Adjust the seasonings and if the sauce is too thin, thicken with a little cornstarch (see page 10 for instructions). Strain through a fine-mesh sieve and set aside until ready to serve.

Prepare the garnish: Just before serving the meal, dip the onion into matzo meal and fry until crisp.

Farfel Kugel

4 servings

A *kugel* is a baked pudding that is served as a side dish at a traditional sabbath dinner. While kugels are often made with potatoes or noodles, this version is made with matzo farfel. *Farfel,* in Jewish cooking, refers to food that is broken into small pieces. You can either purchase a box of matzo farfel or crush sheets of matzo into bits to use in this savory dish.

    ½ onion, minced
    1 stalk celery, finely chopped
    ⅓ cup vegetable shortening
    4 cups matzo farfel
    2 apples (MacIntosh work well), peeled, cored, and diced
    1 teaspoon salt
    ½ teaspoon black pepper
    2 teaspoons paprika
    2 eggs, lightly beaten
    1 cup chicken stock, preferably homemade

Preheat the oven to 350°.

Heat the shortening and sauté the onion and celery until translucent. Add the farfel and apples, mix together, and cook another 2 minutes. Add the salt, pepper, paprika, eggs, and stock, mix together, and simmer 2 minutes. Pour into a greased 9-inch square baking dish and bake 30 minutes until firm. Let sit 20 minutes, cut into squares, and serve.

Honey-glazed Carrots

4 servings

8	carrots
1	tablespoon sugar
1	teaspoon salt
¼	cup honey
¼	cup orange juice, preferably fresh squeezed
½	teaspoon black pepper
¼	teaspoon cardamom
⅛	teaspoon nutmeg

Peel the carrots, cut in half lengthwise, and slice. In a saucepan of boiling water, cook the carrots with sugar and ½ teaspoon salt sbout 6 minutes. Drain and hold in a colander.

In a sauté pan, dissolve the honey in orange juice over medium heat. Reduce to a syrup and add the remaining salt and seasonings. Add the carrots and simmer until heated thoroughly. Set aside until ready to serve.

MAIN COURSE ASSEMBLY: Slice 4 pieces of brisket and place at the bottom of the serving platter at 6 o'clock. Using a slotted spoon, place the carrots to the right at 2 o'clock and the kugel to the left at 11 o'clock. Cover the meat with the sauce and top with fried onions.

Stewed Fruit

4 servings

2	apples (MacIntosh work well)
2	pears
1	orange, peeled
1	cup sugar
2	cups apple juice
1	cup orange juice, preferably fresh squeezed

1 cinnamon stick
1 bay leaf
1 cup chopped walnuts
1 cup prunes
1 cup dried apricots
¼ teaspoon mace
1 tablespoon chopped fresh mint
¼ teaspoon cardamom
1 tablespoon lemon zest (finely grated outer yellow rind, do not use white part)

Peel, core, and dice the apples and pears and place in water until ready to use so they do not turn brown. Drain when ready to use.

With a paring knife, remove the white skin from the peeled orange and remove sections of the orange from the surrounding membrane, making perfect bright-orange wedges.

In a saucepan, combine the sugar, juices, cinnamon stick, and bay leaf. Bring to a boil; then reduce to a simmer. When the liquid becomes syrup, remove the cinnamon stick and bay leaf. Add the fruit, nuts, and seasonings and half the lemon zest.

Serve hot or cold in a glass bowl. Garnish with the remaining lemon zest.

EASTER MENU

Couscous on a Bed of Red and Green Leaf Lettuce
  with Ancho Chili Peppers and Sun-dried Tomatoes

Roast Loin of Pork with Mustard Sauce

Warm Beet Salad with Orange Wedges

Wilted Arugula and Spinach with Smoked Turkey Breast

Raisin and Nut Cake

EASTER IS A TIME OF NEW BEGINNINGS. I remember one Easter in particular. At the time I was living with my cousin Ann. She would see me and cry, "What is wrong? You have a good job, but you can't take care of yourself." I didn't care enough about myself to buy a winter coat. She wanted to help me so very badly, but she couldn't.

I remember when I was at my bottom, living in a single-room occupancy. I was making good money, running a restaurant and catering hall. I chose that place to live because it was the cheapest in the city and I needed to spend every dime I had on booze and drugs. One day a man two doors down died. He was found in his room a couple of days later and I remember them carrying him out stiff as a board. I began to pray, "Please, God, don't let me die in here alone." I kept using and no matter how much I used, I kept crying and praying, "Please don't let me die here alone." He didn't; I got evicted! God did for me what I could not do for myself.

Then I lost my job. So I sold fruits, vegetables, and flowers on the Lower East Side at 1st Street and 1st Avenue. I was standing on the corner asking myself, "What happened?" My dreams of having a family of my own, owning a restaurant, and being a man respected by his peers seemed to vanish. I thought to myself, "Maybe it could be the booze and the drugs!" A moment of clarity, as they say.

My health had also begun to fail, and I ended up in the hospital, where they suggested I go into a detox.

And only when I went to a meeting and saw people struggling just like me and staying clean, did I feel there was a better way. From early recovery until this day, the only chance I felt I had at a good life was to stay clean and sober. When I walked into my first meeting with my cousin Ann, I just knew this was my only shot. I left the detox with only a pair of chef pants, a shirt, and a pair of sneakers to my name. But I felt hope for the very first time in a long while.

While I was using, I was either "poor Gino," or I was hanging around people less fortunate. I was never an equal. Yet from the beginning, when I went to meetings I experienced unconditional love. Not approval or disapproval. Just acceptance. When I first walked in the door they told me to sit down and relax, because I was so very tired.

At my home group they seemed to know what I needed; they left me alone, only suggesting I get a sponsor and keep coming to meetings. I remember I felt crazy, and all they would tell me was that I was doing great and I sounded like I was right where I was supposed to be.

While I was in the detox, a very motherly, heavyset black woman who seemed soft and sincere came to bring meetings to us. She said she couldn't promise me a wife or a job, but that I would get better and feel better. And boy, that sounded good! Whenever I finished talking to her I felt better. Two years into my recovery, she passed on, but I will always remember her. So many people in my early recovery are gone. When I am out jogging, I sometimes picture them there in a cheering section—with all of them waving pennants and wearing baseball caps, cheering me to go a little farther. Without their strength, I could not have done it.

When I think about how fortunate I am to have a second chance at life, I am so very thankful. And what I give back through service, and through my cooking, is my gratitude.

When I think about being reborn, it is exactly what has happened in recovery: a new outlook on life.

Couscous on a Bed of Red and Green Leaf Lettuce with Ancho Chili Peppers and Sun-dried Tomatoes

4 servings

Couscous—a very small wheat pasta—is a staple of North African cooking. Because it absorbs fragrances and flavors so well, it makes a wonderful base for salads like this one.

GREENS
1 head red leaf lettuce
1 head green leaf lettuce

COUSCOUS
5 cups water
2 tablespoons soft butter
1 teaspoon salt
2 cups couscous

DRESSING
3 ancho chili peppers
6 sun-dried tomatoes
¾ cup virgin olive oil
3 garlic cloves, thinly sliced
3 scallions (white part only), thinly sliced
2 tablespoons honey
¼ cup balsamic vinegar
   juice of ½ lemon
1 tablespoon chopped fresh parsley
1 teaspoon salt

Prepare the greens: Remove the outer and blemished leaves from the lettuces. Wash as described on page 10. Tear into 4-inch pieces and toss together. Place in a colander and refrigerate until ready to use.

Prepare the couscous: Bring the water, butter, and salt to a boil; then add the couscous. Turn off the heat immediately and cover without stirring. Wait about 15 minutes. When all the water is absorbed, turn out onto a sheet pan. Fluff with a fork and refrigerate.

Prepare the dressing: In a bowl, cover the chili peppers with hot water to rehydrate them (takes about 5 minutes). Wearing plastic gloves, cut them in half, remove the seeds, and slice lengthwise. Rehydrate the sun-dried tomatoes as you did the chili peppers and thinly slice.

Heat 1 tablespoon olive oil in a small frying pan and simmer the garlic slowly until golden and crisp and pieces are like chips. Reserve the oil.

In a mixing bowl, combine the chili peppers, tomatoes, garlic, scallions, honey, vinegar, lemon juice, parsley, and salt. Let sit for 20 minutes. Whisk vigorously with a wire whisk, slowly adding the olive oil you used to cook the garlic plus the remaining olive oil, making an emulsion. Toss with couscous and refrigerate.

GARNISH
- 1 teaspoon virgin olive oil
- ½ onion, finely chopped
- 1 carrot, peeled and diced
- 1 teaspoon salt
- ½ teaspoon black pepper
- ½ teaspoon sugar
- 1 stalk celery, diced
- 1 medium zucchini, diced
- ½ tomato, diced

Heat the olive oil in a sauté pan and sauté the onion until translucent. Add the carrot and cook over medium heat 3 minutes, stirring occasionally. Add a small amount of seasonings in stages. Each time you add a vegetable, add a little more seasoning. Add the celery and cook another 3 minutes; add a few drops of water to create steam and aid in the cooking. Add the zucchini and tomato, and continue cooking another 3 minutes. Finish seasoning and set aside.

Assemble the dish: Place the lettuce along the bottom of a serving platter. Place the couscous in the center in a mound and sprinkle the cooked vegetables around and over the top, giving contrasting color and texture to the creation.

THE FOLLOWING THREE RECIPES make up the main course in the Easter menu.

Roast Loin of Pork with Mustard Sauce

4 servings

- 4 pounds roast, preferably center cut pork loin
  (ask the butcher to give you the bones also)
- 2 tablespoons virgin olive oil
  juice of 1 lemon
- 4 garlic cloves, minced
- 1 teaspoon salt
- ½ teaspoon black pepper
- ½ teaspoon ground coriander
- 1 teaspoon chili powder
- ½ teaspoon ground cumin
- 2 quarts chicken stock

Preheat the oven to 350°.

Rub the roast with olive oil and then lemon juice. Combine the garlic and seasonings and rub on the roast.

Place the bones in a roasting pan and place the roast on top of the bones. Roast about 1 hour or until the internal temperature shows 140° on a meat thermometer. When the roast is done, set aside in another pan and cover with plastic wrap. The meat should rest about an hour at room temperature; if cut too soon, it will "bleed" too much, losing its natural juices and becoming dry. Natural juices that drip into the pan can be poured into the finished sauce.

Continue roasting the bones until they become brown (about another 20 minutes). Leave the bones in the pan and deglaze with the stock—pour the stock into the pan and cook on stove over high heat, scraping the bottom of the pan with a wooden spoon. When the stock is reduced by half, strain and set aside.

SAUCE
- 1 teaspoon virgin olive oil
- ½ onion, diced
- 3 garlic cloves, chopped
- 1 carrot, diced

1 stalk celery, diced
2 tablespoons canned tomato paste
all of pork stock from earlier in recipe
1 cup cider vinegar
½ cup soy sauce
2 tablespoons Dijon mustard

Heat the olive oil in a sauté pan and sauté the onion and garlic until they caramelize. Add the carrot and celery and continue cooking over medium heat, stirring constantly. When the vegetables are brown, add the tomato paste, continuing to stir. The trick here is patience; making a good sauce takes time. When the tomato paste begins to brown and all the liquid has evaporated, add 1 cup stock. Continue cooking, scraping the browned bits from the bottom, giving the sauce richness and flavor. When all the liquid has evaporated, add another 1 cup stock and repeat the procedure. Add 1 more cup stock and repeat the procedure. When finished, add the vinegar, soy sauce, and mustard, reduce by half, and add the remaining stock. Simmer for 30 minutes.

Depending on the consistency of the sauce, you may need to thicken it with a little cornstarch (see page 10 for instructions). Use your own judgment. When you are happy with the consistency, strain the sauce through a fine-mesh sieve and set aside until ready to serve the rest of the meal. Reheat before serving.

Warm Beet Salad with Orange Wedges

4 servings

5 beets, peeled and thinly sliced
4 oranges, peeled
5 scallions (white part only), thinly sliced
½ tablespoon balsamic vinegar
1 tablespoon virgin olive oil
1 tablespoon fresh grated ginger (or 1 teaspoon ground ginger)
¼ teaspoon cayenne pepper

1 teaspoon salt
½ teaspoon black pepper

Cook the beets in 1 gallon boiling salted water until tender, about 6 minutes; then drain.

With a paring knife, remove the white skin from the peeled oranges and remove the sections of orange from the surrounding membrane, making perfect bright-orange wedges.

Place the beets, orange wedges, scallions, vinegar, olive oil, and seasonings in a mixing bowl and toss gently. Set aside.

Wilted Arugula and Spinach with Smoked Turkey Breast

4 servings

4 bunches arugula, stems removed
4 bunches spinach, stems removed
1 tablespoon virgin olive oil
1 onion, thinly sliced
4 ounces smoked turkey breast, chopped
1 teaspoon salt
½ teaspoon black pepper

Wash the arugula and spinach as described on page 10.

Heat the oil in a skillet and sauté the onion until translucent. Add the turkey and cook 3 minutes over medium heat, stirring occasionally. Add the arugula, spinach, and seasonings and continue cooking until the vegetables are wilted.

MAIN COURSE ASSEMBLY: Slice the pork ½ inch thick. Bring the mustard sauce to a boil and let simmer. Place warm beet salad in the center of a serving platter. To the left, overlap 4 slices of pork atop beets and cover the bottom half of the pork with sauce. Place the wilted arugula and spinach against the beets and to the right of the pork. Make sure the arugula and spinach are well drained before serving.

The natural colors of the ingredients, framed by a white plate, make a beautiful picture.

Raisin and Nut Cake

Makes two 9-inch cakes

CAKE
- 1½ cups lukewarm water
- 2 tablespoons dry yeast
- 2 teaspoons salt
- ½ cup sugar
- 1½ cups shortening
- 5½ cups bread flour

Combine the water and yeast in a mixing bowl. Let stand 10 minutes. Add the salt, sugar, and shortening (reserve 1 tablespoon to grease a second bowl later) to the liquid and ferment 10 minutes. Sift the flour and add to the liquid. Mix 10 minutes at low speed on a mixer with a dough hook. Dust the bowl with flour as you are mixing so the dough does not stick to the sides. If you do not have a mixer, knead by hand 15 minutes.

Place in a bowl greased with shortening. Cover with plastic wrap and let proof (rise) for 1 hour in a warm place.

FILLING
- 1 cup sliced almonds
- 1 cup chopped walnuts
- 1 cup dark raisins
- 1 cup golden raisins
- 1 tablespoon grated lemon peel
- 1 tablespoon grated orange peel

juice of 1 lemon

juice of 1 orange

1 cup fresh breadcrumbs

2 eggs

FINISH

egg wash made with 1 egg and 1 tablespoon water

1 tablespoon butter, melted

¼ cup sugar

1 tablespoon cinnamon

1 tablespoon powdered sugar

Prepare the filling: Preheat the oven to 400°. Roast the almonds and walnuts on a sheet pan for 5 minutes. Rehydrate the raisins about 5 minutes in just enough hot water to cover them. Squeeze out all excess water.

In a mixing bowl, combine the nuts, raisins, lemon and orange peel, lemon and orange juice, breadcrumbs, and 2 eggs. Mix until well blended.

To assemble, turn the dough onto a floured surface and divide in half. Roll the dough into 2 rectangular pieces, each 20 inches long and 10 inches wide. Spread the filling evenly over each piece of dough. Lift the edge farthest from you and roll toward yourself. Just before you are finished completing each roll, brush the end with egg wash and finish the roll, creating a seal at the seam. Cover the remaining egg wash and store in the refrigerator to be used later.

Using two 9-inch springform tube pans sprayed with nonstick coating, place each roll in a pan with the seam side down, pressing the ends of the rolls together to seal. Brush the top of the dough with butter, cover with plastic wrap, and let proof (rise) 1 hour or until double in size.

Preheat the oven to 350°.

Bake each roll, or cake, 15 minutes. Remove from the oven, brush with egg wash, and sprinkle with granulated sugar and half the cinnamon. Finish baking another 20 minutes, remove from the oven, and let cool 30 minutes. Release springform, lift out the cakes, and slide the bottom of pan off. Let cool another 20 minutes. Slice the cakes and dust with the powdered sugar and remaining cinnamon. Serve slightly warm.

MEMORIAL DAY BARBECUE

Orange-Strawberry Salad with Apples and Pears
in a Sweet Yogurt Sauce

Cabbage and Potatoes Braised in Chicken Stock
with East Indian Spices

Sautéed Sugar Snap Peas and Scallions

Tandoori Chicken

Grilled Sirloin on Skewers

Angel Food Cake with Strawberry Glaze

MEMORIAL DAY TRADITIONALLY BRINGS MEMORIES of those who have died defending our country, protecting our freedom, our families, our lives. In my thoughts, I remember the war we fight for our recovery. I remember John, Santos, and Eileen, who fought their war against AIDS.

I have been in recovery for eight years now. There are so many people who have touched my heart who are no longer here. I thought you got clean and everything was perfect. What I found out was that life continues. It seems like I opened my eyes and there was a plague. I didn't know how it started, when or why, just that it was there and most of my friends were touched by it.

I remember visiting my friend John C. in the hospital. I began crying. He said to me, "G (he always called me G), what are you going to do except live?" It seemed apparent that he was going to live life as fully as he could.

We talked about going to Florida and the girls we were going to meet. I talked to John every night, mostly about women! I felt so uncomfortable around women, and I would say, "Did she ask about me?" and he'd say, "Yeah, G, she did" and laugh! I would go out on a date and he would give me instructions on what to do, when to pay for taxis and when not to. It seemed like he knew what he was doing, yet he never made me feel foolish for asking. There was never approval or disapproval, just friendship.

Santos was a fixture at meetings downtown. He was always very loud and enthusiastic about recovery. One day he told me the most courageous thing I could do as an addict was to stay clean. And I knew what he was talking about. I knew what life was like using, but I didn't know what it was like clean, and I was scared. He stayed clean for thirteen years and when his time came, he faced it never picking up. It is something I pray I would be able to do.

My first holiday in recovery, I decided to spend without my family. I was not ready. I was on shaky ground and I decided to hang around the meetings. Eileen asked me if I wanted to go to a sober gathering with her. I was so surprised by her invitation. It made me feel so much a part of the human race. At the gathering there was a feeling of camaraderie. A mix of people who normally would not be socializing together were bonding in a wonderful way. We all were sharing our gratitude for our freedom from the disasters of our lives.

When I think of my friends and the lessons I learned from them, their memories live forever and I am able to share them with others. The three most important things in life are to love, to be loved, and to leave a positive impression on others.

Planted with small trees, the courtyard at Hazelden New York provides a natural backdrop for a relaxing barbecue in the middle of the city.

Orange-Strawberry Salad
with Apples and Pears in a Sweet Yogurt Sauce

4 servings

1 orange, peeled
1 pint strawberries
½ cup dark raisins
½ cup chopped walnuts
1 apple, washed, peeled, cored, and diced
1 pear, washed, peeled, cored, and diced
1 tablespoon honey
  juice of ½ lemon
1 teaspoon hot sauce
½ cup pineapple juice, preferably from concentrate or you can use canned
1 cup plain yogurt (low fat if you prefer)
¼ teaspoon salt
⅛ teaspoon white pepper

Preheat the oven to 400°.

With a paring knife, remove the white skin from the peeled orange and remove sections of orange from the surrounding membrane, making perfect bright-orange wedges.

To wash the strawberries, dip into cold water. Remove the stems and cut berries in half.

Rehydrate the raisins 5 minutes in just enough hot water to cover. Squeeze out excess water.

Place the walnuts on a sheet pan and roast 5 minutes.

In a medium mixing bowl, combine the fruit and nuts. In a large mixing bowl, combine the honey, lemon juice, hot sauce, pineapple juice, and yogurt. Whisk with a wire whisk until well blended. Add the fruit/nut mixture, salt, and pepper, and gently mix. Place in a decorative or glass bowl and serve cold.

Cabbage and Potatoes Braised in Chicken Stock with East Indian Spices

4 servings

½   head green cabbage
5   white potatoes
1   teaspoon virgin olive oil
½   onion, thinly sliced
2   garlic cloves, thinly sliced
1   teaspoon curry powder
½   teaspoon turmeric
½   teaspoon cumin
½   teaspoon chili powder
1   teaspoon salt
½   teaspoon black pepper
2   tablespoons white vinegar
1   tablespoon granulated sugar
2   cups chicken stock, preferably homemade

Wash and core the cabbage; then cut into 2-inch pieces. Peel and slice the potatoes. Keep them submerged in cold water until ready to use. This prevents them from oxidizing and turning brown.

Preheat the oven to 350°.

Heat the oil in a 2-handled saucepan and sauté the onion and garlic until translucent. (You will be adding ingredients, then transferring the pot from the stove to the oven. If you don't have the pot called for, use a pot that is ovenproof.) Add the cabbage and continue cooking for 3 to 4 minutes at medium heat. Add the potatoes, seasoning, vinegar, and sugar and cook another 4 minutes. Add the stock, bring to a boil, cover with lid or aluminum foil, and bake in the oven 20 minutes or until the potatoes are tender.

Place in a bowl and serve warm.

Sautéed Sugar Snap Peas and Scallions

4 servings

- 4 cups sugar snap peas
- 1 bunch scallions
- 1 tablespoon virgin olive oil
- 3 garlic cloves, thinly sliced
- 1 tablespoon soy sauce

Wash the sugar snap peas; then remove the tips and the thick thread that runs down the back of the pod. Leave the peas in the pod.

Remove the root (white part) and half the green part of the scallions.

Heat the olive oil in a sauté pan over high heat, and let it get hot enough to begin to smoke. Add the peas and garlic and sauté for 2 minutes, tossing frequently. Add the scallions and soy sauce and cook another 2 minutes. Serve immediately, so the dish is fresh and hot.

Tandoori Chicken

4 servings

- 1 pound boneless chicken breast, about 4 breast halves
- 1 cup plain yogurt
  juice of ½ lemon
- ⅓ cup tandoori masala (a special mixture of spices you can purchase at an Indian specialty store)
- 1 teaspoon cumin
- 1 teaspoon chili powder
- ½ teaspoon salt
- ¼ teaspoon black pepper
  Mango chutney (you can purchase at an Indian specialty store)

Cut each chicken breast into 4 pieces.

Mix the yogurt, lemon juice, tandoori masala, cumin, chili powder, salt, and pepper in a mixing bowl. Add the chicken and mix until the chicken is evenly coated. Let marinate 2 hours.

If you will be using wooden skewers, soak them in water 2 hours so they will not burn while grilling.

Place 4 pieces of chicken on a skewer, leaving a little space between each piece. Spray your grill with nonstick pan coating and grill about 3 minutes on each side (for a total of 6 minutes). Mango chutney makes a nice accompaniment.

Grilled Sirloin on Skewers

4 servings

> 1   pound top sirloin
> 1   tablespoon grated fresh ginger
> 4   tablespoons soy sauce
> 1   teaspoon cayenne pepper
> 4   tablespoons cider vinegar
> 1   tablespoon sugar

Remove the fat from the sirloin and cube into 2-inch pieces.

Combine the ginger, soy sauce, pepper, vinegar, and sugar in a mixing bowl. Add the sirloin and mix until well coated. Let marinate 2 hours.

If you will be using wooden skewers, soak them in water 2 hours so they will not burn while grilling.

Place sirloin cubes on skewers, leaving a little space between each piece. Spray your grill with nonstick pan coating and grill about 4 minutes on each side (for a total of 8 minutes).

Angel Food Cake with Strawberry Glaze

Makes two 10-inch cakes

I always make two angel food cakes because the ingredients blend better with the increased volume and the result is superb. Plus if I don't need two cakes, I have one in the freezer for a quick dessert.

1 cup cake flour
2 cups sugar
1 cup egg whites
¼ teaspoon lemon juice, preferably fresh squeezed
⅛ teaspoon salt
½ teaspoon vanilla extract
½ teaspoon lemon extract

Preheat the oven to 350°.

In a mixing bowl, sift together the flour and 1 cup sugar; set aside.

Clean a stainless steel bowl with vinegar, and then dry with a paper towel. This is to ensure that the egg whites will peak and expand. If there is any trace of oil on the bowl's surface, the whites will not whip up. Also, you use a stainless steel bowl because any other type of bowl will be too porous and will have absorbed previously used oils. No matter how hard you work at cleaning it, you will never completely remove the oils.

With a mixer, vigorously whip the egg whites until they begin to peak. Then gradually add the lemon juice, salt, and 1 cup sugar. (The acidity of the lemon juice helps stabilize the egg whites.) Continue beating until soft peaks form. Whisk in the vanilla and lemon extracts.

Gently fold in the flour and sugar with a rubber spatula, making sure you do not knock out the air; yet you want the flour/sugar to absorb the egg whites.

Spread into two 10-inch ungreased tube pans. Bake 45 minutes or until a toothpick inserted into the center of each cake comes out dry.

Remove from the oven and let cool on a baking rack 20 minutes. Run a paring knife around the sides and center of the pan. Turn out onto the baking rack and let cool another 20 minutes.

GLAZE

1 pint fresh strawberries
   zest of 1 lemon (see below for method)
1 cup sugar
1 cup orange juice, preferably fresh squeezed
½ cup honey

Dip the strawberries into cold water, letting sand sink to the bottom of the bowl. Remove the stems and cut the berries in half.

To zest a lemon, take a whole lemon and finely grate just the outer yellow rind, making sure you do not use any of the white part.

Heat the sugar in a saucepan over medium heat until it begins to dissolve, stirring with a wooden spoon. Add the orange juice and honey and simmer until the mixture becomes a syrup. Add the strawberries and blend to coat in the syrup.

To serve, slice the angel food cake and spoon glaze over each slice.

THOUGHTS ON RECOVERY

I remember the first time someone called me "Mr. Dalesandro" in recovery. I felt as if I was being acknowledged for the first time. It was the first time someone referred to me in a respectful manner, and I liked the way it felt. For so long I had treated myself badly.

When I came into recovery, friends and family saw I was trying to take care of myself; they were happy for me and respected what I was doing.

A lot of my friends asked me if I was afraid of breaking my anonymity by writing about my life. My response was, "Anyone who knows and cares about me says, 'Thank God he is in recovery!'" When I was in treatment, a nurse asked me what I was going to do when I left. And I realized it was up to me.

I remember one time when I was using, I was sitting on a bench and a woman was afraid to sit next to me because of the way I looked. And now my appearance is totally different. I feel like I have a presence that exemplifies self-respect. I never got this from a drink or a drug.

My wife says I'm a *mensch*, which is all I ever wanted to be, a good guy.

Hector Matos always goes all-out loading the salad bar with the freshest summer vegetables and crisp salads.

Summer

*Fresh herbs preserved in olive oil
add character and summer sunlight
to any dish you make.*

Roasted Pepper with Goat Cheese Pizza

Grilled Chicken Breast with Cilantro Pesto,
Sweet and Spicy Corn,
and Seared Polenta with Sun-dried Tomatoes
and Black Sicilian Olives

SUMMER BRUNCH

Scrambled Eggs with Chili and Cheese
Sliced Tomatoes with Fresh Basil
Chocolate Chip Muffins

Home Fries
Fresh Peaches and Raspberries with Yogurt

When I think of summer, I think of how powerful the creative force is. Everything seems to be intensified. The sun is so strong, with its bright light shining on us. One of the things I enjoy most is sitting on the beach watching the tide come in and go out. The tide has so much power, and I can do nothing to alter its flow.

My wife, Laurie, and I often go to Maine during the summer, and we stay in a small town on the coast. I am always amazed by the natural beauty. It is as though God is an artist who is showing me this beautiful painting. The sun, stars, clouds, beaches, and rocks seem as if they are placed there for me to witness. At night, I lie in bed next to Laurie and I can hear the ocean waves hitting the beach. They seem so powerful, yet I feel safe. I feel so insignificant, yet significant. I feel so much a part of the picture that I am almost overwhelmed by the moment. Some moments are magic, and this is one. I look forward to others. What I experience is hope, something I never had when using.

The summer always makes me feel primitive. I don't know if it is the hot days or the sun or the warm nights. The produce in the markets is bright, full, and sweet, just like my wife! People wear fewer clothes and you can see them more clearly. You can see the natural beauty of your surroundings and the people. The recipes I cook seem to become more and more simple as the days go by. I feel so stimulated and I have to conserve my energy.

Summer is a time of growth. The market displays an abundance of produce nurtured by the sun's strength. The grass grows quickly and tall and the trees grow thick with rich green leaves. Roses and many other flowers bloom in the summer, sharing their glorious colors and fragrances.

The produce of summer is special—nothing beats a fresh tomato in August. Vine-ripened melons are sweet as sugar, and the scent of fresh basil fills the air. Big, fat peaches with their fuzzy coating and sweet plums with their tangy skins are treasures.

The abundance of summer reminds me of the growth I experience in recovery. The seeds that were planted in early recovery begin to take root and grow. After a hard examination of myself and working at accepting who I am, I can then take action, moving forward, making decisions for the long haul, not the quick fix. In recovery I've learned to act in ways that I respect, trying to be the person I was meant to be. I now am able to grow in ways that were not possible while I was actively using.

I remember the time my cousin Phil came to me for a job. Wherever I worked, Phil would come to work with me. Basically, I liked having a family member around; someone I trusted to be loyal. And I took advantage of the relationship. I had him do things that put his job in jeopardy.

When I had three years clean and sober, Phil came to me again looking for a job. But this time, instead of giving him a job, I took him to a meeting. He now has five years sober and is following his own dreams, working in health care.

I learned that the amends I make in Step 9 do not mean simply saying "I'm sorry" when I'm ready to, but truly making amends, setting things right, when God gives me an opportunity to act in a loving way. It's up to me to change my behavior and do the right thing.

When I was using, I was one sorry addict; I was always saying "I'm sorry." When I made amends to my cousin, I didn't say I was sorry; I said I had a disease and couldn't be there. Given an opportunity, I told him I would like to take part in a relationship as an equal. Step 9 helped us end the isolation and have relationships in the moment without the baggage of the past.

I remember when I was using and my mom was sick. I prayed for her not to die because I knew I couldn't be there for her. She got better and she saw me clean and was very happy. When she passed, I was able to show up for her as her only son, in a responsible way. Not having to live with that guilt has freed me, and it is all possible because of the program, my family, and my friends.

The Summer Market

When I was growing up, there was always a garden in our backyard. It amazed me how much produce we were able to get from such a small garden. The men in our family took great pride in what they grew.

I remembered that garden recently when Laurie and I went to my Uncle Roland and Aunt Connie's home in Canarsie. The first thing Uncle Roland did was take Laurie and me out to the garden to show off his squash and tomatoes. He would show us what was newly planted, what was blooming, and where he planned to add his next crop. He would always talk about how his squash was bigger and better than his neighbor's. He was in love with his garden.

In the part of Italy where my family was from, you could not own the land or the produce grown on it. You were granted a certain amount by the landlord.

So one of the first things my family did when they got to America was plant a garden. I believe the reason Italian immigrants liked to work for themselves, owning their own businesses, is that they wanted to be independent and not controlled by anyone else. There is a saying, "Who could govern the Italians and who would want to!"

Laurie's father, too, whose parents came from Eastern Europe, loved his garden and fruit trees. After World War II, one of the few things the Soviet government allowed people to keep for their own use was the produce grown in their victory gardens. One way a totalitarian state tries to break down the spirit of the people is by not allowing them to have their own personal relationship with the land. Land is seized in the name of the governing power and the people lose their spiritual connection with the creative force. In much the same way, alcohol robs alcoholics. We lose our connection to ourselves, our surroundings, and the creative force. But our difficulties have left a fertile place in our hearts where the seed of recovery can be planted, and we can grow our own spiritual connection with our Higher Power.

BASIL You cannot talk about the summer market without first mentioning basil. It comes to the market in mid-June and is available throughout the season. It seems to take over the market. Its aroma permeates the air, and its rich green color decorates every stand. Deeply rooted in Mediterranean cooking, basil has a sweet and spicy flavor. It is used to enhance, not dominate, its companion ingredients.

When picking out basil, use smell as the best indicator of potency. Crumble a few leaves in your fingers and smell the aroma. It should be strong and fresh. The leaves should be bright green and the stems should not be wilted.

Basil should be cut just before using because its oils will run out, reducing its potency and causing it to lose its freshness. Never chop it, either finely or coarsely, or cut in strips, because the heat from the knife will release its juices.

Fresh herbs are usually used late in the cooking process because their flavors are released right away. Dried herbs are used in the beginning of the cooking process because they need to be rehydrated before they can release their flavors.

To store basil and all fresh herbs, wrap them in a damp paper towel placed in a plastic bag. Store herbs in the coldest part of your refrigerator (about 40 to 45 degrees). They should be used within a week.

CORN To pick out good corn make sure the ears are full, husks are green, and tassels are brown. There are many good varieties of sweet corn available from June through September.

Corn, ideally, should be cooked the same day it is picked. It is far better to purchase corn from roadside stands or farmers markets because it will be fresher. One of the advantages of the newer varieties is its extended shelf life. Some varieties can last up to six days in the refrigerator. My favorite is a hybrid variety called Diablo. You can find Diablo in the market the last two weeks of August through the first two weeks of September. Hybrid varieties can be very difficult to grow, making the crop inconsistent and more of a risk for the farmer. There is less chance of hybrids reaching the market than typical varieties. The birds, the bugs, everyone loves them because of their sweetness!

Every year there are new varieties on the market. The newer varieties tend to be crisper and candy sweet. Years ago, the corn was more creamy (less crisp) and less sweet. It had a more earthy flavor. One of the reasons I like Diablo is that the kernels are crisp but not overly sweet. It's up to you, what you like.

EGGPLANT Eggplants are so beautiful that many people grow them as ornamental plants. Laurie tells me about watching eggplants grow in her father's garden. First come the beautiful purple flowers. Then a tiny dark purple ball forms where the bloom has been. Every day the eggplant grows bigger and more beautiful, taking on its amazing shape. It is like watching a miracle occur right before your eyes. Laurie says that eggplants are possible only from God's soil and her father's love.

When you select eggplants in the market, they should be firm, heavy for their size, and free of blemishes. Oversized eggplants tend to be bitter. The skin should be glossy and deep purple in color. They come into season late July and stay through late October. They are best stored uncovered in the refrigerator and can last up to one week.

Eggplant tends to be bitter later in the season. I like to sprinkle eggplant slices with salt, place them in a colander, and put a weight on top to squeeze out the bitter juices. You can use plates and heavy cans as weights. Eggplants are excellent in meatless recipes because of their full-bodied texture. At home, during the summer, we used to eat eggplant six different ways! My favorite was braised with tomato sauce tossed with fettuccine and black Sicilian olives with a piece of semolina Italian bread.

PEPPERS Peppers originated in the Caribbean, grown by the indigenous people. They have become a staple globally. You can find them in markets all over the world.

Bell Peppers are best when fully developed and firm, with a thick flesh, shiny skin, and uniform color. Peppers can be stored in a paper bag in the refrigerator for three to five days. Red and yellow peppers will not store as long as green peppers because they are more fully ripened.

Bell peppers come to the market in early summer, with green peppers being the first crop. Later on in the season, red and yellow peppers begin to arrive. Green peppers are more assertive than red or yellow and in many ways are the best to cook with. I like to use red and yellow peppers in salads; the bright colors are more visually appealing, and they are sweeter and juicier than the green. Bell peppers are great used in combination with other vegetables in pastas, stews, and medleys.

Bell peppers are very versatile; you can sauté, stew, steam, bake, roast, or smoke them. I like to place them over an open flame, char them, cut them into quarters, and remove the seeds. Toss with Kalamata olives, feta cheese, and fresh basil. Drizzle with olive oil and a few drops of fresh lemon juice.

Chili Peppers are related to the bell peppers but are much spicier. Most of their heat comes from their seeds and the oils of their flesh. They are referred to as "the berry that bites back"! The available variety of chili peppers is vast. They are widely used throughout the world, but some of the more common chili peppers available in the United States include ancho, jalapeño, chipotle (smoked jalapeño), and serrano chili peppers. Chili peppers are smaller than the bell pepper, with thinner flesh and sometimes wrinkled skin. They are available both fresh and dried. When you choose fresh chili peppers, look for blemish-free peppers with shiny skins and attached stems.

Chilies are an excellent flavoring agent in cooking, allowing you to reduce the amount of fat used because of the richness of their flavor. They also make excellent decorations. There is a saying, "Never trust those who eat their decorations," but I have always loved to decorate my kitchen with beautiful foods. Their colors and shapes are art, in and of themselves, and they give the impression of abundance and create an earthy feel that soothes all they surround.

TO ROAST PEPPERS: Rub the skin of the peppers with olive oil. Grill them over a very hot barbecue grill or use tongs and cook them over the open flame of the stove. Turn the peppers so they are blistered on all sides. Afterward, place them in a paper bag and close. Let them stand until they are cool. Peel off the skin and run the peppers under cold water. Cut them into ½-inch strips.

SNAP BEANS There is a large variety of snap beans. Three types readily available at the market are string beans, flat beans, and roma beans. They come in different colors, textures, and shapes. Their colors vary from deep rich green to yellow to purple, their textures from tender to chewy. When selecting beans at the farmers market, ask if they were handpicked. Always choose handpicked beans when you can get them. You want the beans to be as uniform in size as possible; machine-picked beans vary greatly in size and flavor, and their handling is often too rough. You may also get hard, overdeveloped beans and the pod will not have its fresh snap. Beans should snap in half when bent. They are available from July through September.

When boiling beans, use a lot of water with a little salt. As beans cook, they release acids into the water; using a large volume of water dilutes the acids and keeps them from breaking down the color of the beans. The salt helps balance the pH of the water. As soon as the beans are cooked, shock them in ice-cold water, drain, and use them in whatever you are preparing. Never sauté beans over high heat because they will lose their taste and color.

String Beans come in a variety of colors: green, yellow, purple. They originated from the tiny, tender French *haricot vert*, a long, pencil-thin pod whose bean is not developed. Multicolored string beans make a beautiful backdrop to grilled tuna with Niçoise olives and a mustard vinaigrette.

Flat Beans look very much like string beans but are flatter and longer. One of my favorite ways to use flat beans in a salad is to combine them with sliced new potatoes and tomato wedges tossed with basil oil and fresh-squeezed lemon juice.

Roma Beans are rounder than string beans and sometimes the pods are spotted with white. They are more chewy, with larger beans within the pod. They are an Italian string bean, and, like Italians, they are more rounded than most! The beans, because of their higher starch content, are best used in stews and sauces. A traditional way to enjoy cooked roma beans is to toss them in tomato sauce, served with freshly grated Pecorino Romano cheese. Cousin Phil called us while we were writing about beans. He told us he likes his beans crisp with oil and garlic, lots of garlic.

SUMMER SQUASH There are many varieties of summer squash: zucchini, yellow squash, straightneck, crookneck, patty pan. Their mild flavor and varying shapes and colors enhance a multitude of dishes.

When picking out squash, select small ones rather than large, because summer squash lose flavor with size. They should be heavy for their size, with no blemishes or soft spots and with a tender skin. Refrigerate squash in an airtight container for three to four days. They come into the market mid-August and stay through October.

One of my favorite ways to prepare squash is to thinly slice them and sauté the slices in olive oil with sliced garlic until they are soft. Then I deglaze them with balsamic vinegar.

TOMATOES Tomatoes are at the heart of southern Italian cuisine. The tomato exemplifies summer. The deep red color and sweet flavor come straight from the hot summer sun. I find any excuse to use them fresh when they are at their peak of flavor in the summertime. In other seasons, I prefer to use canned, because nothing compares to a vine-ripened tomato. Locally grown tomatoes are always best. Transported tomatoes are picked and shipped green so they do not bruise, then "gassed" to produce their red color. They are frequently lacking in taste, to put it mildly.

Tomatoes come to the market in mid-July and stay through September, peaking in August. They are so wonderful; there is nothing better than sliced tomatoes with fresh basil and virgin olive oil. They are the simplest of foods and, eaten at the right time, make a perfect summer appetizer.

The best tomatoes have a deep, even, red color, although more and more you are seeing different varieties of tomatoes with vibrant colors that range from yellow to orange. A good tomato should be plump and unblemished and have a sweet aroma. Store tomatoes in a cool, dark place, but not in the refrigerator where the ripening process is slowed and the flesh becomes coarse.

There are many varieties of tomatoes. The beefsteak is perfect sliced and eaten raw. Plum tomatoes have more pulp so are good for canning and making sauce. Most people do not think of cooking with cherry tomatoes. Yellow and orange cherry tomatoes are actually very good to sauté and add to any medley of summer vegetables because they are less juicy and have more pulp than red cherry tomatoes. They add flavor, texture, and color. Red cherry tomatoes are great in salads.

FLAVORED OILS

Roasted Garlic Oil and Roasted Garlic Paste

Basil Oil

Cilantro Oil

Dill Oil

Rosemary Oil

Lemon Oil

Orange Oil

Chili Oil

I STARTED MAKING FLAVORED OILS IN MY KITCHEN when I wanted to enhance my recipes with a perfect balance between my two favorite ingredients: fresh herbs and olive oil. Infused oils allow you to enjoy the elegant flavors of summer after the weather turns cold and fresh herbs are hard to find. Now I look for any excuse to use flavored oils in the foods I prepare.

Flavored oil enhances whatever you are making, giving a burst of flavor without adding a lot of calories. When you use flavored oils, you do not have to prepare rich sauces or meats with a high-fat content. You can choose leaner cuts of meat and get your flavor and richness from a monounsaturated fat that helps lower your cholesterol.

Flavored oils are great in just about anything. When you cook with infused oils, the flavors are dispersed throughout the dish and stay with the food longer. Adding flavored oils to a finished dish gives a fresh taste that is immediately apparent. They can be used as a marinade for grilling or as an addition to soups, stews, and sauces. They make a great butter substitute on bread. Or they can just be drizzled over a finished dish, giving it a simple elegance.

The ingredients in flavored oils have to be of the highest quality; otherwise the oil will absorb unpleasant characteristics. The herbs should be freshly picked and gently washed, and the oil should be fresh and clean tasting.

When making flavored oils, use an oil that does not have a distinct flavor. You want to *accompany* the flavoring, not dominate it. I use virgin olive oil, which has a less dominant flavor than extra virgin olive oil. Olive oil picks up all the flavors with which it is combined, making it perfect for flavored oils.

I like to prepare herb-infused oil the old-fashioned way. I add the herbs to the oil, let it stand a week, then strain through a fine-mesh sieve to remove the herbs. This will improve the oil's longevity. The only way to really know whether the oil has absorbed enough flavor is to taste it. If it tastes right to you, it's ready. Depending on the intensity of flavor I want, either stronger or milder, I increase or reduce the amount of herbs. Heat intensifies the flavor and speeds up the process, so if I want finished flavored oil more quickly, I heat the oil before adding the herbs.

Preparing flavored oils is not an exact science. A lot depends on the type of oil, the herb, the time of the season, and the variety. You will have to experiment. And remember, there is no right or wrong.

When using flavored oils, always remember: This is about fun! It is up to you what combinations you prepare or what you use them in.

OLIVE OIL Not all olive oil is the same. There are different grades of olive oils— extra virgin olive oil, virgin olive oil, olive oil, and pomace oil. The grades depend on the acidity level and the process by which the oil is extracted.

Extra virgin olive oil is extracted mechanically from the first pressing, with an acidity level under 1 percent. It has a distinctive flavor ranging from mild to peppery, depending on where the olives were grown, when they were harvested, and how the oil was extracted.

Virgin olive oil is from the second pressing. It has its own individual taste, milder than extra virgin olive oil. It is higher in acidity, 1 to 3 percent.

Olive oil is a blend of the third pressing of the olives with the addition of extra virgin olive oil to cover up its imperfections. It has a 5 to 10 percent acidity level.

Pomace oil is extracted with solvents and is also blended with a higher quality olive oil. It is the most neutral in flavor, virtually tasteless, the least expensive, with the highest acidity level. It is usually used for frying.

I almost always use virgin olive oil. I won't use any other grade of olive oil unless I am frying.

For really good olive oil, the olives have to be of the highest quality, picked at the peak of ripeness, with no bruises; otherwise they begin to oxidize, which raises the acidity level of the oil. After the olives are picked, they are made into a paste using one of two methods. The first is to crush the olives slowly between two rotating stones, mixing them into a paste; the second is to use something called a hammer mill, which crushes the olives before they are mixed into a paste.

In traditional olive-oil making, the liquid of the olives is separated by spreading the paste onto mats and then pressing with a press. As more pressure is applied, the oil and water are removed by centrifuge, producing extra virgin olive oil. As the pressure is increased, the oil becomes higher in acidity. The result of this second pressing is virgin olive oil. On the third pressing, the oil is refined, corrected for flavor, acidity, and color, and is called olive oil. The oil that remains is extracted with solvents and filtered, resulting in a bright, clear oil. This oil has no taste and is odorless and sold as pomace oil. Pomace oil is sometimes marketed as "light olive oil," but don't be fooled. It has the same fat content as any oil. The sellers just want to charge you more for an inferior oil.

Olive oil is considered a fruit juice and is very perishable. Look for bottles that have harvest dates. You should have oil that was made no more than two years ago. The best way to store olive oil is in a cool, dark place. Don't let it just sit on your shelf; you should use it as soon as possible.

Roasted Garlic Oil and Roasted Garlic Paste

Yield: 2 cups oil and ½ cup paste

This is a great recipe, because you get two wonderful condiments at once—roasted garlic oil and roasted garlic paste. Roasted garlic paste adds a superb flavor to soups, stews, sauces, and salad dressings. It has a sweet, mild taste that does not overpower the other flavors it accompanies. Roasted garlic oil is a wonderful flavoring agent, and you can use it in many ways. I especially like it on grilled vegetables in the summer. The roasted garlic helps cut the acidity in the oil.

    10 heads of garlic
     2 cups virgin olive oil
        salt and black pepper to taste

Preheat the oven to 375°. Slice off the top third of each head of garlic (the pointed end), slicing through the tops of the cloves. Peel off the papery outer layers of skin and place the garlic heads cut sides up to fit in a shallow baking dish. Pour the olive oil over the garlic and season with salt and pepper. Cover with aluminum foil and bake until the cloves begin to pop out of their skins, about 1 hour. Uncover and bake another 15 minutes until the garlic begins to caramelize and turn a rich golden color.

Strain the baking oil through a fine-mesh sieve and cheesecloth. (Make sure to rinse the cheesecloth before you pour the oil through so you don't wind up with a lot of lint.) Store in a glass jar; use within 2 to 3 weeks.

To make the paste, squeeze the cloves out of the skin and mash. You can store the paste 2 or 3 days refrigerated in a glass jar. I like to spread the garlic paste on focaccia with goat cheese and green and black olives.

GARLIC *Word of garlic's healing properties has been handed down by priests and physicians for thousands of years. Garlic is an antispasmodic. It stimulates the activity of the digestive organs and relieves various problems associated with poor digestion. It also helps in bringing down fevers, thins the blood, and improves circulation.*

Garlic is helpful for all intestinal infections, including dysentery, cholera, and typhoid. It prevents and relieves chronic bronchitis. A mere half clove a day can rev up the blood-clot-dissolving activity that helps prevent heart attacks. My grandmother even told us that garlic could ward off evil spirits!

Basil Oil

Yield: 4 cups

I like the flavor of my oils extracted delicately, letting the flavor of the herb bloom. The oils give any dish a distinct, fresh flavor. When making basil oil or any delicate herb oil, such as cilantro, tarragon, or chervil, you can skip the step of heating the oil if you prefer a lighter and milder flavor. Just place the herbs in the jar with the oil and let stand for a week.

> 4 cups virgin olive oil
> 3 cups fresh basil leaves, washed and stemmed

Place the oil in a pan, heat to 160°, and add the basil leaves. Remove the pan from the stove and let stand 20 minutes. Pour into a glass jar, seal, and let stand for 1 week.

Strain the oil through a sieve to remove the herbs. Pour the oil into a decorative bottle with a seal. You can add a fresh sprig of basil to the bottle to make it more decorative as well as help you identify the oil. Use as needed. The oil can be stored for up to 3 weeks.

VARIATIONS

Cilantro oil: Substitute 3 cups fresh cilantro for the basil.

Dill oil: Substitute 3 cups fresh dill for the basil and reduce the olive oil to 2 cups.

Rosemary oil: Substitute 4 cups fresh rosemary for the basil.

Lemon oil: Substitute the zest of 6 lemons for the basil and reduce the olive oil to 2 cups. To zest lemons, finely grate the outermost yellow rind, making sure not to use the bitter white membrane underneath.

Orange oil: Substitute the zest of 3 oranges for the basil leaves and reduce the olive oil to 2 cups.

Chili oil: You can experiment using a combination of chili peppers—smoked, dried, or fresh—whatever you have available. Substitute 10 dried serrano chili peppers, seeded and chopped, and reduce the olive oil to 2 cups; or try 8 smoky chipotle peppers. Chili oil lasts longer than herb and citrus oils because the flavors do not evaporate but develop over time. Use within 6 weeks.

PESTO

Basil Pesto

Cilantro Pesto

Dill Pesto

Sun-dried Tomato Pesto

Tarragon Pesto

IN MY KITCHEN I ALWAYS have plenty of pesto around. This fragrant mixture of finely chopped herbs, olive oil, and other flavor-intense ingredients is a staple in my cooking. What I like to do in the height of summer is pick out the freshest and most aromatic herbs and make them into pesto. I freeze the pesto in small plastic containers, and, later in the year when fresh herbs are no longer available, I can thaw the pesto and add a touch of summer to whatever I am making.

A lot of Italian cooking involves finding ways to preserve the freshness of the season. The quality of what's available in the market determines what you put on your menu. During the olive harvest, for example, some of the olives are stored in brine to be eaten later in the year. The rest are used to make olive oil. This is the natural way to preserve what the creative force has given us.

Pesto and flavored oils capture the essence of the ingredients; they combine those ingredients in ways that make them easier for us to use. They can add character and fortitude to any dish you make, especially in dark winter months, when you really need to feel some summer sunlight.

Basil Pesto

Yield: 4 cups

- ½ cup pine nuts
- 2 large bunches fresh basil leaves, washed and stemmed (about 4 cups, loosely packed)
- 3 garlic cloves, coarsely chopped
- 2 cups virgin olive oil
  pinch of salt and black pepper
- ½ cup freshly grated Pecorino Romano cheese

Preheat the oven to 400°.

Roast the pine nuts on a baking sheet in the oven until golden, about 5 minutes.

Place the basil in the work bowl of a food processor and begin processing. Add the garlic, then pine nuts, and continue processing. When the mixture has a grainy, pastelike consistency, begin adding the oil a little at a time, continuing to process. Wait until the oil is absorbed before adding the next small amount. Add salt and pepper. When all the oil is added and absorbed, add the cheese. As soon as the cheese is mixed in, stop processing; if you overprocess, the cheese will melt.

Place in containers, seal, and label. You can use your pesto immediately or store it up to 6 months in the freezer. Pesto stored in the refrigerator will last up to 1 month.

Cilantro Pesto

Yield: 4 cups

- 2 dried ancho peppers
- 1 cup coarsely chopped walnuts
- 4 bunches fresh cilantro, washed and stemmed (3 cups, loosely packed)
- 2 garlic cloves, coarsely chopped
- 2 cups virgin olive oil
  pinch of salt and black pepper

Preheat the oven to 400°.

Wearing plastic gloves, split the ancho peppers in half, remove the seeds, and coarsely chop.

Place the walnuts on a baking sheet and roast in the oven about 5 minutes, until you can smell their nutty aroma and they turn a rich golden brown.

Place the cilantro leaves in the work bowl of a food processor and begin processing. Add the garlic, walnuts, and ancho peppers and continue to process. When the mixture has a rough, pastelike consistency, begin adding the oil a little at a time, continuing to process. Wait for the oil to be absorbed before adding the next small amount. Add salt and pepper. When all the oil is added and absorbed, stop processing.

Place in containers, seal, and label. You can use your pesto immediately or store it up to 6 months in the freezer. Pesto stored in the refrigerator will last up to 1 month.

Dill Pesto

Yield: 6 cups

> 2 bunches fresh dill leaves, washed and stemmed (about 2 cups, loosely packed)
> 1 garlic clove, coarsely chopped
> 2 cups black Kalamata olives, pitted (see page 103)
> 2 cups virgin olive oil
> ½ cup feta cheese

Place the dill in the work bowl of a food processor and begin processing. Add the garlic and olives and continue to process. When the mixture reaches a pastelike consistency, begin adding the oil a little at a time, continuing to process. Wait for each dab of oil to be absorbed before adding the next small amount. When all the oil is added and absorbed, add the feta cheese and process just enough to combine the cheese with the paste.

Place in containers, seal, and label. You can use your pesto immediately or store it up to 6 months in the freezer. Pesto stored in the refrigerator will last up to 1 month.

Sun-dried Tomato Pesto

Yield: 6 cups

> 2 cups sun-dried tomatoes
> 1 cup pine nuts
> 2 bunches fresh parsley, washed and stemmed (about 2 cups)
> 2 garlic cloves, coarsely chopped
> 2 cups virgin olive oil
>   pinch of salt and black pepper

Preheat the oven to 400°.

Rehydrate the sun-dried tomatoes 2 to 3 minutes in enough hot water to cover. Drain, squeeze out the excess water, and pat dry.

Roast the pine nuts in the oven on a baking sheet until they are golden, about 5 minutes.

Place the sun-dried tomatoes and parsley in the work bowl of a food processor and begin processing. Add the pine nuts and garlic and continue to process. When the mixture has a rough, pastelike consistency, begin adding the oil a little at a time, continuing to process. Wait for each dab of oil to be absorbed before adding more. Add salt and pepper. When all the oil is added and absorbed, stop processing.

Place in containers, seal, and label. You can use your pesto immediately or store it up to 6 months in the freezer. Pesto stored in the refrigerator will last up to 1 month.

Tarragon Pesto

Yield: 4 cups

> 1 cup sliced almonds
> 2 bunches fresh tarragon, washed and stemmed (about 1 cup)
> 2 bunches fresh parsley, washed and stemmed (about 2 cups)
> 2 garlic cloves, coarsely chopped
> 2 cups virgin olive oil
>   pinch of salt and black pepper

Preheat the oven to 400°.

Place the almonds on a baking sheet and roast in the oven until golden, about 5 minutes.

Place the tarragon and parsley in the work bowl of a food processor and begin processing. Add the almonds and garlic and continue to process. When the mixture has a pastelike consistency, begin adding the oil a little at a time, while continuing to process. Wait for the oil to be absorbed before adding the next small amount. Add salt and pepper to taste. When all the oil is added and absorbed, stop processing.

Place in containers, seal, and label. You can use your pesto immediately or store it up to 6 months in the freezer. Pesto stored in the refrigerator will last up to 1 month.

SUMMER ENTRÉES

*Rigatoni with Sautéed Arugula, Roasted Peppers,
    and Grilled Chicken*

*Shrimp and White Bean Casserole with Wheatberries,
    Diced Tomatoes, and Fresh Basil*

Marinated Lamb Medallions on a Bed of Grilled Vegetables

*Grilled Chicken Breast with Cilantro Pesto,
    Sweet and Spicy Corn, and Seared Polenta with
    Sun-dried Tomatoes and Black Sicilian Olives*

*Sautéed Fillet of Sole with Cucumber and Lemon Oil,
    Sautéed Zucchini with Basil Pesto, and Braised Eggplant*

Rigatoni with Sautéed Arugula, Roasted Peppers, and Grilled Chicken

4 servings

1 pound boneless chicken breast (about 4 breast halves)
1 cup virgin olive oil
   salt and black pepper to taste
1 tablespoon chopped fresh thyme
1 tablespoon salt
1 pound rigatoni
1 cup sliced onion
1 tablespoon chopped garlic
4 cups arugula, washed and stemmed
1 medium red pepper, roasted (see page 77)
1 medium yellow pepper, roasted (see page 77)
   sprigs of thyme (for garnish)
   grated Parmesan cheese (for garnish)

Prepare the chicken: Clean any fat and gristle from the chicken breast. Cut into 2-inch cubes. Place in a bowl, toss with ¼ cup of the olive oil, and sprinkle with a pinch of salt and pepper and half the chopped thyme. Let marinate 2 hours in the refrigerator.

Heat the grill. When hot, brush the grate with olive oil and place the chicken on it. Brown on both sides until cooked. Make sure the chicken is not overcooked; it should be moist and tender.

Prepare the rigatoni: Fill a large stockpot with 1 gallon water, and add 1 tablespoon salt and 1 tablespoon of the olive oil. Bring to a rapid boil. Add the rigatoni and cook until the pasta is soft and chewable, but still firm to the teeth. Reserve ¼ cup of the pasta water.

Prepare the sauce: While the pasta is cooking, sauté the onion in a large frying pan with the rest of the olive oil until the onion is translucent. Add the chopped garlic and continue cooking until the garlic gives off a nice, sweet aroma. Add the arugula, roasted peppers, and grilled chicken.

Assemble the dish: Toss the cooked pasta, ¼ cup of the pasta water, and the remaining chopped thyme with the sauce. Divide among 4 pasta bowls. Garnish with sprigs of thyme and grated Parmesan cheese.

Shrimp and White Bean Casserole with Wheatberries, Diced Tomatoes, and Fresh Basil

4 servings

This is a typical Mediterranean-style entrée. The shrimp is combined with beans, grain, and vegetables to provide a complete meal. Wheatberries are among my favorite whole grains. They are the whole wheat kernel and have a wonderful chewy texture. Using seasonal tomatoes and basil finished with virgin olive oil gives a perfect balance to the dish. All your nutritional needs are met in one entrée.

1 cup white beans, soaked in water overnight (see note)
1 cup dried wheatberries, soaked in water overnight (see note)
2 tablespoons salt
2 bay leaves
2 whole cloves
1 pound raw shrimp, peeled and deveined
½ cup virgin olive oil
1 cup diced onion
¼ cup chopped garlic
2 tomatoes, diced
1 cup fresh basil leaves, cut into thin strips
¼ cup lemon juice, preferably fresh squeezed

Drain the soaked white beans and wheatberries. Place in two separate stockpots, cover with water, and add 1 tablespoon salt, 1 bay leaf, and 1 clove to each pot. Bring the water to a boil, turn down the heat, and let simmer for 1½ hours, until the beans and wheatberries are soft but still chewy. When they are fully cooked, strain the beans and wheatberries from the broth, reserving 2 cups of the white bean broth for later use.

> *TO CLEAN SHRIMP before you cook, simply pull off the legs at the center of the shrimp, then pull the shell away. (The shells can be saved for making shrimp stock or shrimp bisque on page 197.) Devein the shrimp by running a small paring knife along the back of each shrimp, making a slit deep enough to expose the vein. Place under cold running water while you remove the vein. Place on dry paper towel and pat dry.*

Heat all but 1 tablespoon of the olive oil in a large saucepan and sauté the onions and garlic until the mixture just turns golden brown. Add the shrimp and continue cooking 3 to 4 minutes. Make sure the shrimp are opaque and not overcooked.

Add the tomatoes, white beans, wheatberries, and ¾ cup of the basil leaves. Add the 2 cups reserved white bean broth. Cook 7 to 10 minutes. Add the lemon juice. This entrée should be a little soupy. Serve in shallow soup bowls. Garnish with the reserved basil leaves and drizzle with the remaining tablespoon of olive oil.

NOTE: Soaking the beans and wheatberries speeds up their cooking and ensures they cook evenly. If you forget to soak them overnight, or if you don't have time, you can omit the step and boil them a little longer, but the result won't be quite the same. If they aren't soaked, the outside cooks too fast and becomes mushy while the center remains hard.

Marinated Lamb Medallions on a Bed of Grilled Vegetables

4 servings

A few applewood chips give the meat a sweet, smoky flavor.

MARINATED LAMB
1½ pounds lamb loin from the saddle, cut into 2-ounce medallions
2 tablespoons rosemary oil (see page 84) or virgin olive oil
juice of ½ lemon
¼ teaspoon salt
⅛ teaspoon black pepper
1 teaspoon chopped fresh rosemary

GRILLED VEGETABLES
1 medium eggplant
2 tablespoons chili oil (see page 84)
juice of ½ lemon
½ cup sun-dried tomato pesto (see page 88)
4 tablespoons balsamic vinegar

¼ teaspoon salt
⅛ teaspoon black pepper
1 zucchini
1 yellow squash
1 red bell pepper
1 yellow bell pepper

Prepare the lamb: Trim excess fat from the lamb. Combine the rosemary oil, lemon juice, salt, pepper, and rosemary in a bowl. Rub the lamb with the meat marinade and let stand 1 hour. Discard marinade.

Prepare the vegetables: Peel the eggplant and cut into slices ¼ inch thick. Layer the slices in a colander, sprinkle with salt, and place a weight on top. I use a few plates with a large can of tomatoes as a weight. This squeezes out the bitter juices. Let the eggplant sit about 1 hour.

Meanwhile, combine the chili oil, lemon juice, pesto, vinegar, salt, and pepper in a large mixing bowl. Cut the zucchini and yellow squash into slices ¼ inch thick. Seed and quarter the red and yellow bell peppers. Toss the zucchini, yellow squash, and peppers in the vegetable marinade and let stand 45 minutes.

Light your grill. When the coals are red hot and a layer of ash has formed over them, brush a clean grate with olive oil. Grill the lamb. It's easier than most people think to make those great diagonal grill marks on your meat. The trick is that once you've placed the meat on the grill, do not handle it for 2 minutes. Let it cook; then turn the meat 180° and the grill will sear a crisscross pattern on it. Grill another 2 minutes without moving it; then turn the meat over, repeating this procedure.

Remove the vegetables from the marinade and reserve the marinade. Place the vegetables in a grilling basket and grill over high heat for 2 minutes on each side. Make sure the vegetables remain crisp. (If you prefer, you can roast the vegetables quickly under a broiler.)

Brush the eggplant with the reserved vegetable marinade and grill for 2 minutes on each side. (I brush the eggplant with the marinade rather than soaking it because eggplant is greedy—it will soak up as much marinade as you can give it.)

Assemble the dish: In a mixing bowl, toss all the grilled vegetables together. Divide the vegetables among 4 plates. Lean the grilled lamb medallions against the vegetables and drizzle with the remaining vegetable marinade.

Grilled Chicken Breast with Cilantro Pesto, Sweet and Spicy Corn, and Seared Polenta with Sun-dried Tomatoes and Black Sicilian Olives

4 servings

I love this dish in part because it contains fresh corn, one of the most incredible tastes of summer. Sure, using frozen corn kernels would be easier than cutting them from the ears, but don't give in to the temptation. The fresh corn is incomparable, plus it's kind of fun to cut the kernels from the ears.

GRILLED CHICKEN BREAST WITH CILANTRO PESTO

1   pounds boneless chicken breast (about 4 breast halves)
1   tablespoon virgin olive oil
    juice of ½ lemon
2   tablespoons balsamic vinegar
    pinch of salt and black pepper
1   cup cilantro pesto (see page 86)
1   tablespoon cilantro oil (see page 84) or virgin olive oil

Remove the fat and skin from the chicken breasts and cut in half. Whisk together the olive oil, lemon juice, vinegar, salt and pepper, and ¾ cup of the cilantro pesto. Rub onto each chicken breast and let marinate 45 minutes.

Grill the chicken breasts at high heat about 6 minutes on each side. Remove from the grill and brush with the remaining ¼ cup of cilantro pesto.

SWEET AND SPICY CORN

4   ears of corn (about 3 cups cut corn)
3   dried serrano chili peppers
1   teaspoon virgin olive oil
½   red onion, diced
1   tablespoon roasted garlic paste (see page 83)
2   tablespoons sugar
1   red bell pepper, diced
1   green bell pepper, diced
2   teaspoons chili oil (see page 84)
1   tablespoon chopped Italian parsley
    juice of ½ lemon

Remove the husks and silk from the corn. Run a paring knife down the cob, cutting off the kernels. Do this in a large mixing bowl because the kernels will fly all over the kitchen!

Rehydrate the serrano peppers about 10 minutes in just enough hot water to cover them. Drain. Using gloves, split in half, remove seeds, and chop.

In a large sauté pan, heat the olive oil and sauté the onion until translucent. Add the garlic paste and sugar, continuing to cook until the sugar is dissolved. Add the corn kernels, bell peppers, and serrano peppers. Continue cooking 4 to 6 minutes until the corn is tender. Add the chili oil, parsley, and lemon juice. Set aside until ready to serve.

SEARED POLENTA WITH SUN-DRIED TOMATOES AND BLACK SICILIAN OLIVES

1 cup sun-dried tomatoes
1½ cups chicken stock, preferably homemade (or 1½ cups water}
1 cup yellow cornmeal
1 tablespoon basil oil or olive oil
1 cup black Sicilian olives, pitted and chopped (see page 103)
1 tablespoon chopped fresh basil leaves
1 sprig fresh cilantro

Rehydrate the sun-dried tomatoes for 20 minutes in just enough hot water to cover them. Drain and chop. Spray a large baking pan with nonstick spray.

In a heavy saucepan, bring the stock to a boil. Add the cornmeal in a slow, steady stream, stirring constantly with a wooden spoon. Crush any lumps against the side of the pot. When the mixture begins to thicken, add the basil oil, olives, sun-dried tomatoes, and fresh basil. When more fully thickened so that a spoon will stand in it, pour the mixture into a greased 8-inch square baking pan or casserole dish so it is about 2 inches in depth. Chill in the refrigerator until firm (about 45 minutes).

Preheat the oven to 350°.

With a cookie cutter, cut the polenta into 3-inch circles. In a nonstick frying pan with a coating of nonstick spray, brown the polenta circles on both sides and then place in the oven for 3 minutes, making sure they are hot throughout.

Assemble the dish: Place the polenta in the center of a serving platter. Arrange the corn around the polenta and place the chicken on top. Drizzle with cilantro oil and garnish with a sprig of fresh cilantro.

Sautéed Fillet of Sole with Cucumber and Lemon Oil, Sautéed Zucchini with Basil Pesto, and Braised Eggplant

4 servings

SAUTÉED FILLET OF SOLE WITH CUCUMBER AND LEMON OIL

2 large eggs
   salt and black pepper to taste
3 cups fresh breadcrumbs (see note on page 27)
1 tablespoon chopped Italian parsley
4 cucumbers
2 tablespoons virgin olive oil
4 4-ounce fillets of sole
1 tablespoon chopped fresh dill
1 tablespoon lemon oil (see page 84)

In a bowl, whisk the eggs and add a pinch of salt and pepper. On a separate plate, combine the breadcrumbs and parsley. Dip the sole first in the eggs and then in the breadcrumb mixture. Set aside.

Peel the cucumbers, cut them in half lengthwise, and remove the seeds with a spoon. Thinly slice the cucumbers.

Heat 1 tablespoon olive oil in a large sauté pan and sauté the sole over medium heat. Cook 4 minutes per side, or until golden brown. Set aside.

Heat the other tablespoon of olive oil in the same sauté pan over medium heat and add the cucumbers. Simmer about 4 minutes. Toss in the dill, and add salt and pepper to taste.

Spoon the sautéed cucumber over the sole and drizzle with lemon oil.

SAUTÉED ZUCCHINI WITH BASIL PESTO

4 medium zucchini
1 tablespoon virgin olive oil
½ onion, thinly sliced
½ cup basil pesto (see page 86)
  salt and black pepper to taste

Wipe the zucchini with a damp towel and slice ¼ inch thick.

Heat the olive oil in the sauté pan and sauté the onion over medium heat until translucent. Add the sliced zucchini and cook about 3 minutes. Add the pesto and salt and pepper to taste, toss, and continue cooking another 2 minutes. Set aside.

BRAISED EGGPLANT

1 medium eggplant
1 tablespoon virgin olive oil
½ onion, diced
  salt and black pepper to taste
1 red bell pepper, diced
1 yellow bell pepper, diced
2 fresh tomatoes, diced
1 tablespoon roasted garlic oil (see page 83)

Peel and dice the eggplant. Place in a colander and weight down (with a few plates and a large can of tomatoes or anything else that works!) to squeeze out the bitter juices.

Heat the olive oil in the sauté pan and sauté the onion until translucent. Add the diced eggplant and a pinch of salt and black pepper. Drizzle a little water into the pan to create steam. Continue cooking about 3 minutes, stirring occasionally. Add the diced peppers and tomatoes. Cook about 2 minutes; then drizzle with the garlic oil.

Assemble the dish: Place the sole along the bottom of a serving platter. Place the zucchini at 2 o'clock and the eggplant at 11 o'clock.

PIZZA

Basic Pizza Dough

Tomato, Basil, and Mozzarella

Barbecued Chicken with Cheddar Cheese

Olive and Feta Cheese

Roasted Pepper with Goat Cheese

Summer Vegetables with Basil Pesto

Deep-dish

PIZZA IS A TRADITIONAL ITALIAN FOOD that lends itself to many untraditional meals. You can combine ingredients in thousands of different ways to make a pizza to your liking.

Pizzas range in style from simple to elegant and everything in between. I like the informality of the way pizza is usually served—family style, in the center of the table with everyone reaching in to pick out a special piece with favorite toppings. There is a special closeness we get with everyone at the table eating from the same pie.

And preparing homemade pizza can be just as much fun as eating it. When I was growing up, everyone in my family had their own favorite pizza combination. It was like a signature; you could tell who made the pie by its topping.

The recipes I provide here will give you a starting point. With a good basic crust recipe and an understanding of the simple cooking techniques, anyone can create a masterpiece by adding different herbs, vegetables, sauces, meats, fruits, and cheeses.

I LIKE TO COOK MY PIZZAS and many of my breads on unglazed quarry tiles that I bought at a tile shop. I simply arrange the quarry tiles on a heavy baking sheet and put them in when I preheat the oven. Cooking on quarry tiles gives the pizza a real pizzeria effect with a crisp crust. You can also use a baking stone like those that are sold in cooking stores, but the advantage of using quarry tiles is that you can create a larger cooking surface for less money.

The trick to cooking pizzas at home is getting them into the oven. With this in mind, the other piece of kitchen equipment that comes in handy when making pizzas is a pizza peel, a long-handled wooden board like those used in pizzerias everywhere. A pizza peel helps you get the pizza in and out of the oven without spilling the topping or burning yourself. If you don't have a pizza peel, you can use a cake circle, a piece of cardboard, or another long, thin object. To use a peel (or one of the alternatives), dust the surface with cornmeal and lay your untopped pizza crust on it. Arrange the toppings on the pizza crust. Then lift the peel with the pizza, bring it to the oven, and slide the pizza off the peel and on top of the quarry tiles in one smooth motion.

Basic Pizza Dough

Yield: Four 6-inch pizzas

2	tablespoons yeast
1¾	cups lukewarm water
2	tablespoons virgin olive oil
2	teaspoons sugar
2	teaspoons salt
4	cups bread flour
1	cup whole wheat flour
	bread flour for dusting during mixing
	cornmeal for dusting work area

In the mixing bowl of a stand mixer, combine the yeast and water and let ferment for 10 minutes until the mixture becomes frothy. Add the olive oil, sugar, and salt and let ferment another 10 minutes.

Sift together the bread and wheat flours. Add the flour to the liquid and mix 10 minutes with a dough hook. Add extra bread flour as needed to keep the dough from sticking to the sides of the mixing bowl.

Place the dough in a greased mixing bowl, cover with plastic wrap, and let proof (rise) 1 hour.

Turn the dough out onto a work area dusted with cornmeal. Divide the dough into 4 equal pieces. Knead into balls; then roll with a rolling pin into rounds 6 inches across and ¼ inch thick. You are ready for toppings!

NOTE: Place a baking stone or quarry tile on a sheet pan in the oven to preheat. Be sure the tile is very hot before placing the pizzas on it. You can tell if the pizza is ready by lifting up the crust with a spatula and seeing if it is browned and crisp. Let cool 10 minutes on a baking rack; then serve.

Tomato, Basil, and Mozzarella Pizza

	pizza crusts (see page 100)
6	tomatoes
1	tablespoon virgin olive oil
½	onion, diced
2	garlic cloves, minced
½	cup fresh basil, chopped
	salt and black pepper to taste
2	cups grated mozzarella cheese

Bring a large saucepan of water to boil. Cut an X on the bottom of each tomato. Boil the tomatoes 3 minutes. Remove from the water and plunge into ice water. When the tomatoes are cooled, peel away the skin. Slice in half, squeeze out the seeds, and coarsely chop.

Heat the olive oil in a sauté pan and sauté the onion and garlic over medium heat until translucent. Add the tomatoes and basil and cook 6 to 8 minutes. Drain the tomatoes and spread over the pizza shells. Add salt and pepper to taste. Top with the mozzarella cheese.

Preheat the oven to 400° and bake 20 minutes.

Barbecued Chicken Pizza with Cheddar Cheese

      pizza crusts (see page 100)
½   **pound boneless chicken breast, about 1 whole breast**
1   **cup barbecue sauce** (see page 118) **or use your favorite purchased sauce**
4   **tomatoes, diced**
1   **tablespoon chopped fresh cilantro**
2   **tablespoons roasted garlic oil** (see page 83)
      salt and black pepper to taste
2   **cups grated cheddar cheese**

Preheat the oven to 400°.

Remove the fat and skin from the chicken and separate the breast. Rub ½ cup of the barbecue sauce onto the chicken and grill, or pan sear, 3 minutes on each side. Slice the chicken breast on an angle and set aside until ready to assemble the pizzas.

In a small bowl, mix the tomatoes with the cilantro and garlic oil.

Dust a pizza peel (or a large cake circle) with cornmeal and place a rolled out crust on top. Spread a layer of barbecue sauce over the crust and top with one quarter of the sliced chicken. Use a slotted spoon to add one quarter of the tomato mixture, and top with one quarter of the cheddar cheese. Slide the pizza from the peel directly onto the hot quarry tiles in the oven. Repeat this procedure for the remaining 3 crusts.

Bake about 20 minutes.

Olive and Feta Cheese Pizza

     pizza crusts (see page 100)
4 cups Kalamata olives, pitted and chopped
2 cups feta cheese
3 tablespoons roasted garlic oil (see page 83)
1 tablespoon chopped fresh dill

Preheat the oven to 400°.

Spread the olives over the pizza shells and crumble the cheese on top. Drizzle with 2 tablespoons of the garlic oil. Bake 20 minutes. After baking, finish with the rest of the garlic oil and garnish with the dill.

NOTE: To pit the olives, rinse and pat dry. Place on top of a kitchen towel and hit each olive with a mallet. This will break the skin, making it easier to remove the pit. The towel cushions the blow, so you won't smash the flesh. Chop the olives coarsely.

Roasted Pepper with Goat Cheese Pizza

     pizza crusts (see page 100)
2 red bell peppers, roasted
2 yellow bell peppers, roasted
4 tablespoons cilantro oil (see page 84)
1 tablespoon chopped fresh cilantro
     juice of ½ lemon
     salt and black pepper to taste
2 ounces goat cheese

To roast peppers, see page 77.

Preheat the oven to 400°.

Combine the roasted peppers with the cilantro oil, chopped cilantro, lemon juice, salt, and pepper. Spread over the pizza shells and then crumble goat cheese over the tops. Bake 20 minutes.

Summer Vegetables with Basil Pesto Pizza

  pizza crusts (see page 100)
1 small pink eggplant
1 tablespoon virgin olive oil
½ onion, sliced
1 yellow squash, thinly sliced
1 zucchini, thinly sliced
1 tomato, diced
½ cup basil pesto (see page 86)
  salt and black pepper to taste

Peel and slice the eggplant. Place in a colander with a weight (a few plates with a large can of tomatoes or anything else that works!) on top to squeeze out the bitter juices.

Heat the oil in a sauté pan and sauté the onion over medium heat until translucent. Add the eggplant and sauté another 2 or 3 minutes. Add the sliced yellow squash and zucchini, tomato, pesto, salt, and pepper. Continue cooking until the vegetables are tender but still crisp. Drain the excess liquid in a colander and spread the topping on the pizza shells.

Bake at 400° for 20 minutes.

Deep-dish Pizza

Yield: Three 10-inch pizzas

This pizza is very good and a lot of fun to eat. When preparing this dish, I think of my cousin Jimmy, pulling at the long strands of cheese, making a mess. With each dish comes a memory and the chance to create another.

  2 tablespoons dry yeast
1¾ cups lukewarm water
⅓ cup honey
  1 tablespoon virgin olive oil
  1 tablespoon salt

1 tablespoon sugar

½ cup powdered buttermilk (makes the dough softer and a little sour)

3 tablespoons chili powder

1 tablespoon black pepper

5 cups bread flour, sifted

extra bread flour for dusting

In the mixing bowl of a stand mixer, dissolve the yeast in water and let ferment 10 minutes.

Add the honey, olive oil, salt, sugar, powdered buttermilk, chili powder, and black pepper to the yeast and water and let ferment another 10 minutes.

Add the flour and mix with a dough hook 10 minutes at low speed. Dust with extra bread flour every few minutes, making sure the dough does not stick to the sides of the bowl. Remove the dough from the mixer, place in an oiled bowl, and cover with plastic wrap. Let rise 1 hour or until it doubles in size.

Brush three 10-inch cake pans with olive oil.

Turn the dough out onto a floured work area. Divide into 3 equal pieces. Knead each piece into a ball and then roll into a 10-inch circle. Place each circle of dough inside a cake pan, and let proof (rise) 30 minutes. Using your fingertips, press lightly on the dough, making dimples.

RICOTTA CHEESE FILLING

2 cups ricotta cheese, drained (placed in strainer overnight)

1 egg yolk

1 teaspoon oregano

pinch of salt and black pepper

Combine the ricotta cheese, egg yolk, oregano, salt, and pepper in a bowl. Spread the mixture in a thin, even layer over the prepared pizza dough.

Preheat the oven to 350°.

PIZZA SAUCE

1 tablespoon virgin olive oil

1 onion, thinly sliced

2 garlic cloves, thinly sliced

4 tomatoes, peeled and seeded (see page 160)
1 cup sliced mushrooms
1 tablespoon dried basil
  salt and black pepper to taste
3 cups grated mozzarella cheese
1 cup grated Parmesan cheese

Heat the olive oil and sauté the onion and garlic until golden. Add the tomatoes, mushrooms, basil, salt, and pepper, and cook over medium heat for 10 minutes. Drain the excess liquid. Spread the mixture on top of the ricotta cheese mixture and bake 20 minutes.

Remove the pizzas from the oven and top with grated mozzarella and Parmesan cheese. Bake another 20 minutes or until golden. Remove the pizzas from the oven and let cool 10 minutes; then remove from the cake pans. Place the pizzas on a baking rack and let cool another 10 minutes. This will give the cheese time to set, so when the pizzas are cut the cheese will not run all over the place.

SUMMER BRUNCH

Scrambled Eggs with Chili and Cheese

Home Fries

Sliced Tomatoes with Fresh Basil

Chocolate Chip Muffins

Fresh Peaches and Raspberries with Yogurt

THERE IS SOMETHING SO NICE about having friends stay overnight and having brunch with them the next day. At times, a couple Laurie has known since college travel down from upstate New York with their two daughters to sleep over. It's like a pajama party! It feels so exciting; why, I don't know. Having friends over seems so intimate. Everyone trying to get cozy in our little five-room apartment. There is so much you can't plan on, like enough blankets or pillows, and inevitably you wind up going out in the middle of the night for something so important that Aurora and Sierra desperately need *now*. In the morning, the girls fight over who is going to work with me in the kitchen. I love the attention. I find something for each of them to do, each task being just as important as the other. They stand on chairs and one mixes the muffin batter and the other scrambles the eggs. Forget about trying to get everyone settled down! Once we all sit down to eat, it seems as if a calm comes over us; we relax and make the plans for the day. Our hearty brunch gives us the energy to keep up with two vibrant girls (we wonder how Lori and Rich do it for the other 364 days!).

Scrambled Eggs with Chili and Cheese

4 servings

12 large eggs
 salt and black pepper to taste
 2 ancho chili peppers
 ½ tablespoon virgin olive oil
 1 green bell pepper, diced
 4 scallions (white and firm green parts), thinly sliced
 1½ cups grated Monterey Jack cheese
 ½ tablespoon chili oil (see page 84)

Whisk the eggs in a mixing bowl with a pinch of salt and black pepper.

Rehydrate the ancho chilies 10 minutes in just enough hot water to cover them. Wearing plastic gloves, split the peppers in half, remove the seeds, and cut into strips. Set aside.

Heat a heavy skillet, add the olive oil and green pepper, and cook until tender over medium heat. Add the scallions and cook another 2 minutes. Pour in the eggs, stirring occasionally. When the eggs begin to thicken, add the ancho chilies and cheese. Continue cooking until the eggs are firm enough for your liking.

Spoon onto 4 plates and drizzle with a little chili oil.

Home Fries

4 servings

4 russet potatoes
 ½ tablespoon virgin olive oil
 ½ onion, thinly sliced
 1 teaspoon paprika
 ¼ teaspoon chili powder
 salt and black pepper to taste

Preheat the oven to 400°.

Bake the potatoes 45 minutes. Remove from the oven and let cool until you are able to handle them. Peel and slice ¼ inch thick.

In a heavy skillet, heat the olive oil and add the onion. Cook over medium heat until translucent. Add the potatoes and continue cooking until they begin to brown. Add the paprika, chili powder, salt, and pepper, and continue cooking until the potatoes are a red-golden brown.

Sliced Tomatoes with Fresh Basil

4 servings

- 4 medium-large tomatoes
- 1 tablespoon fresh basil leaves, washed and patted dry
- 1 tablespoon roasted garlic oil (see page 83)
   salt and black pepper to taste

Slice the tomatoes ¼ inch thick and overlap the slices on a plate.

Slice the basil leaves into strips and sprinkle over the tomatoes. Drizzle with garlic oil. Season with salt and pepper.

Chocolate Chip Muffins

Makes 12 muffins

- 2 cups all-purpose flour
- ½ cup granulated sugar
- ½ cup light brown sugar, packed
- 1 tablespoon baking powder
- ¼ teaspoon salt
- 1 cup milk
- 1 egg

½   cup melted butter
1   cup chocolate chips

Preheat the oven to 400° and spray 12 muffin cups with nonstick spray or line with paper liners.

Mix the flour, sugar, brown sugar, baking powder, and salt in a bowl. In a separate bowl, mix the milk, egg, and melted butter. Combine the mixtures and fold in half the chocolate chips.

Spoon into the prepared muffin tins. Sprinkle the remaining chocolate chips on top of the muffins and bake 20 minutes.

To test whether the muffins are done, insert a toothpick into the center. If done, the toothpick should come out clean.

Fresh Peaches and Raspberries with Yogurt

4 servings

4   peaches
2   pints raspberries
1   cup plain yogurt
2   tablespoons honey
¼   teaspoon cinnamon

Wash the peaches, cut them in half, remove the pits, and thinly slice.

Pick through the raspberries to remove the damaged berries. Combine the fresh, plump raspberries with the sliced peaches, making sure to be very gentle with the berries as they bruise easily.

In another bowl, whisk together the yogurt, honey, and cinnamon. Refrigerate the fruit and yogurt separately until ready to serve.

To serve, dish the fruit onto a plate and spoon a dollop of yogurt over it.

SUMMER BARBECUE

Grilled Salmon, Onions, and Mushrooms

Grilled Eggplant and Zucchini

Tomatoes Stuffed with Bulgur Wheat and Summer Vegetables

Wilted Arugula with Lemon Oil

Upside-down Plum Cake

MY WIFE, LAURIE, grew up on Long Island and comes from a family that has always been big on barbecues. Her father would try to barbecue just about any-thing—at least once. His favorite was lamb shish kebab. He would treat his coals with such care, fanning them until they were red-hot, and then letting them form a layer of ash, just right for even heating.

A barbecue was a real family event—everyone was part of the team. The whole family helped cart the food, dishes, and utensils to the picnic table. Mom would marinate the meat and vegetables; her sister, Suzan, would make the salad; Laurie and Neal, her brother, would peel the local corn, while Dad, of course, was king of the barbecue.

Now during the hot summer, Laurie and I look forward to leaving the city. On a leisurely drive along the south shore of Long Island, we pick up fresh fish and produce. Barbecues are special. Less formal than other meals, everyone can relax, slow down, and take the time to prepare the simple foods that we crave on a hot summer day.

Grilled Salmon, Onions, and Mushrooms

4 servings

4 4-ounce salmon fillets
3 teaspoons lemon oil (see page 84)
   a few pinches of salt
10 large white mushrooms
   juice of 1 lemon
2 teaspoons roasted garlic oil (see page 83)
   a few pinches of black pepper
2 red onions
2 teaspoons virgin olive oil

Brush the salmon with 2 teaspoons of the lemon oil, sprinkle with a pinch of salt, and let stand 20 minutes.

Wipe the mushrooms clean and cut away the stems. Squeeze the lemon juice over the mushrooms, brush with the roasted garlic oil, and sprinkle with a little salt and pepper.

Cut the onions into slices ½ inch thick. Brush with the olive oil and sprinkle with salt and pepper.

Grill the onions 2 to 3 minutes on both sides over medium-hot coals. When they begin to caramelize, remove from the grill and place on a platter.

Place the fillets in the center of the grill skin side up with the mushrooms around them. Grill the salmon 4 minutes on each side. The salmon should still be pink in the middle when you remove it from the grill. Arrange the salmon on top of the onions. Top with the grilled mushrooms and drizzle with the remaining teaspoon of lemon oil. This makes a simple and beautiful entrée.

Grilled Eggplant and Zucchini

4 servings

- 2 medium eggplants, peeled and sliced ½ inch thick
- ½ teaspoon salt
- 2 tomatoes, washed and sliced ½ inch thick
- 2 medium zucchini, washed and sliced ½ inch thick
- ½ cup basil oil (see page 83)
- 4 tablespoons virgin olive oil
- ½ cup basil pesto (see page 86)
- juice of ½ lemon
- ⅛ teaspoon black pepper

Peel the eggplants and slice ½ inch thick. Rub the slices with salt and place in a colander and weight down with any heavy object to squeeze out the bitter juices. Let stand 1 hour.

Combine the eggplants, tomatoes, and zucchini, and rub with the basil oil and olive oil. Grill the tomatoes 1 minute on each side, the zucchini 2 minutes on each side, and the eggplant 3 minutes on each side. When done, place the vegetables in a mixing bowl and add the pesto, lemon juice, and pepper. Mix well and serve hot.

Tomatoes Stuffed with Bulgur Wheat and Summer Vegetables

6 servings

- ½ pound bulgur wheat
- 6 tomatoes
- ¾ teaspoon salt
- 4 tablespoons roasted garlic oil (see page 83)
- ½ onion, finely diced
- 2 carrots, finely diced
- 4 large white mushrooms, diced (about 1 cup)

        1 zucchini, finely diced
    ⅛ teaspoon black pepper
        1 tablespoon chopped fresh dill (reserve sprig for garnish)
           juice of ½ lemon

In a pot of salted boiling water, cook the bulgur wheat 25 minutes or until tender. Drain and set aside.

Slice the tops off the tomatoes and reserve. Hollow out the tomatoes with a melon scoop, reserving the pulp. Make sure you do not pierce the skin of the tomatoes as you are scooping out the pulp. Sprinkle the hollow tomatoes with ½ teaspoon of the salt and drizzle with 2 tablespoons of the garlic oil. Set aside.

Preheat the oven to 350°.

To prepare the filling, heat 1 tablespoon of the garlic oil and sauté the onion until translucent. Add the carrots and continue cooking over medium heat until the carrots begin to soften. Add the mushrooms and season with a pinch of salt and pepper. Continue cooking 2 to 3 minutes. Add the zucchini and reserved tomato pulp. Season with another pinch of salt and pepper, and simmer 4 minutes. Add the dill and cooked bulgur wheat. Stir and cook another 3 to 4 minutes. Finish with the lemon juice and let cool.

When the filling has cooled, spoon it into the tomato shells. Place the stuffed tomatoes in a baking dish, drizzle with the remaining garlic oil, and replace the tops of the tomatoes. Bake 20 minutes. Place on a serving platter and garnish with sprigs of fresh dill.

Wilted Arugula with Lemon Oil

4 servings

        1 tablespoon virgin olive oil
        2 garlic cloves, thinly sliced
        6 bunches arugula, washed and stemmed
           salt and black pepper to taste
        1 tablespoon lemon oil (see page 84)
        1 tablespoon chopped Italian parsley

In a sauté pan, heat the olive oil and sauté the garlic until it becomes golden and crisp (like chips). Add the arugula, salt, and pepper, and continue cooking until the greens are completely wilted, about 2 to 3 minutes. Lift the arugula from the pan with tongs, squeezing out excess water, and place the arugula on a serving platter. Drizzle with the lemon oil and garnish with Italian parsley.

Upside-down Plum Cake

Makes one 10-inch cake

6	plums
1½	cups brown sugar, packed
1	cup butter, room temperature
3	cups sugar
4	eggs
4	cups cake flour
2	tablespoons baking powder
1½	cups milk
2	tablespoons vanilla extract
½	cup apricot glaze (can be purchased at any gourmet shop)
	powdered sugar for dusting

Cut the plums in half, remove the pits, and thinly slice. Combine with 1 cup of the brown sugar and set aside, allowing the plums to develop character.

In a stand mixer with paddle attachment, cream together the butter and granulated sugar at medium speed. When the mixture is smooth, add the eggs 1 at a time.

Preheat the oven to 350°.

Sift together the flour and baking powder. Add half the dry ingredients to the batter, and then half the milk and vanilla. Mix until incorporated, and add the rest of the dry ingredients and then the rest of the milk and vanilla. Mix only until all the ingredients are dispersed evenly.

Spray a springform pan with nonstick coating. Line the bottom of the pan with the remaining ½ cup of brown sugar. Layer the sliced plums on the sugar and then pour the batter over the plums. Bake 45 minutes or until an inserted toothpick comes out clean.

When the cake is done, remove from the oven and let cool 20 minutes. When it is still warm, release the sides of the springform pan and remove them. Place a cake circle or a platter over the cake and turn it over onto the circle. Remove the bottom of the springform pan *very* gently. Be careful not to damage the top of the cake.

Melt the apricot glaze with a little water in a saucepan. Brush the glaze over the top of the cake. Dust with powdered sugar and serve warm.

INDEPENDENCE DAY MENU

Pulled Pork Loin with Barbecue Sauce

Jicama and Green Cabbage Coleslaw

Black-eyed Peas with Basmati Rice

Barbecued Corn on the Cob

Fresh Watermelon

TO MANY PEOPLE IN RECOVERY, Independence Day has a double meaning. Now that I'm sober, I am finally independent, free of any substance that ever ruled me. The fireworks I see today are real, not some drug-induced hallucination. There is such power in knowing who I am. By helping me connect with a Higher Power, the Twelve Steps offer a strength I never experienced while using. I always believed that I had to have the answers, but now I am more comfortable not knowing. With recovery at the center of my thoughts and actions, I know I will have a useful and purposeful life.

As I celebrate Independence Day, then, I think of my breaking free of the grip of addiction, just as the original thirteen colonies broke free of British rule. Yet even after winning their independence, the colonies didn't each go their separate ways. They needed to cooperate and collaborate with each other for support, and we, too, have to rely on others—family, friends, co-workers, and neighbors. We remain interconnected.

So this Fourth of July, celebrate your own independence while you celebrate this country that has brought together people from all over the world. Share this classically American menu with people you care about.

Pulled Pork Loin with Barbecue Sauce

4 servings

1 8-pound pork butt
1 lemon, cut in half
¼ cup chili oil (see page 84)
½ cup cilantro pesto (see page 86)
1 teaspoon salt

Rub the meat with the lemon halves, squeezing out the juice as you rub. Rub with the oil, then the pesto, and sprinkle with salt. Let marinate 2 hours.

BARBECUE SAUCE
1 cup ketchup
1 cup chili sauce
2 tablespoons chipotle oil (see page 84)
½ cup apple cider
⅓ cup molasses
¼ cup espresso or strong coffee
1 tablespoon Dijon mustard
½ teaspoon cayenne pepper
1 teaspoon salt
½ teaspoon black pepper
   hickory chips to throw in with the coals

Combine all the barbecue sauce ingredients in a mixing bowl and whisk until well combined.

Light the coals in the grill. When they become white, spread the coals and put a roasting pan half filled with water directly on top of the coals. Place the rack about 2 inches above the pan of water, place the meat on the rack, and cover. Cook the meat for 2 hours, turning every 30 minutes. After the first hour, brush the meat every 15 minutes on all sides with the barbecue sauce. During the last 10 minutes of cooking, add a few hickory chips to the coals. These will start to smoke, giving the meat a smoky, hickory flavor.

When finished, the meat will be nice and tender. Remove it from the grill and place on a cutting board. With a fork, pull the meat apart, brush with the barbecue sauce, and serve on soft rolls.

Jicama and Green Cabbage Coleslaw

4 servings

Jicama is a tuberous vegetable grown mainly in Mexico. With a tan skin and white interior flesh, it looks a little like a large, round potato, but the taste is quite different. It is wonderfully crisp and juicy and sweet, and an excellent accompaniment on a raw vegetable platter, in salad, or in this coleslaw. Jicama is widely available in grocery stores.

- ½ head green cabbage, cored and shredded
- 2 medium jicama, peeled and cut into thin strips
- 2 carrots, peeled and grated
- 1 cup plain yogurt
- 1 tablespoon lemon oil (see page 84)
- 1 tablespoon chopped fresh dill
- ½ teaspoon salt
- ¼ teaspoon black pepper
- 2 teaspoons vinegar
- 1 teaspoon sugar

Wash, core, and shred the cabbage. Steam 2 minutes, drain, and squeeze out the bitter juices.

Add the jicama and carrots and mix together. Mix in the yogurt, lemon oil, dill, salt, pepper, vinegar, and sugar, and refrigerate. When chilled, serve in a decorative bowl.

Black-eyed Peas with Basmati Rice

4 servings

Basmati rice has a natural nutty flavor that makes it ten times more aromatic than either brown or white rice. This rice cooks fast and is very tender.

- 1 cup black-eyed peas, soaked overnight
- ½ teaspoon salt
- 2 bay leaves

1	cup basmati rice, rinsed under cold water
1½	cups chicken stock, preferably homemade
2	red peppers, diced
2	tomatoes, diced
½	red onion, diced
3	tablespoons dill oil (see page 84)
½	teaspoon hot sauce
	juice of 1 lemon
1	tablespoon chopped fresh parsley
¼	teaspoon black pepper

Cook the black-eyed peas in boiling water with ¼ teaspoon of the salt and 1 bay leaf until tender, about 1 hour. Drain and cool in refrigerator.

In a saucepan, combine the rice, chicken stock, remaining ¼ teaspoon of salt, and remaining bay leaf. Bring to a boil, reduce the heat to simmer, and cover. When all the liquid is absorbed, about 15 minutes, turn out into a bowl and fluff up with a fork. Place in the refrigerator to cool.

When the rice and peas are cool, combine them in a large mixing bowl (remove the bay leaves), tossing them together. Add the red peppers, tomatoes, onion, dill oil, hot sauce, lemon juice, parsley, and pepper. Toss lightly and chill 2 hours. Serve when well chilled.

Barbecued Corn on the Cob

4 servings

4	ears of corn with husks intact
2	tablespoons chili oil (see page 84)

Soak the corn in their husks in water and 1 tablespoon of the chili oil for 2 hours. Remove the outer layer of husks from the cob, and peel back the inner layer of husks and the silk. Brush with the remaining chili oil; then pull the husks back up, so the cob is covered.

Place on the grill and roast 20 minutes. The moist husks and hot oil combine to make sweet, hot, and tender corn that only you and God can create!

Fresh Watermelon

Simply slice the watermelon and place on a platter. There will be none left by the end of your barbecue.

Choosing Melons

Melon comes into the market in late July and stays through September. There is nothing as naturally sweet and juicy. When melons are ripe, they fall from the stem. Never pick out a melon that has its stem attached because that means it was picked too early. When it is ripe, it falls from the vine on its own.

CANTALOUPE AND MUSKMELON When choosing a cantaloupe or muskmelon, look to see that the skin on one of its sides is turning from green to yellow. The melon should have a sweet smell. When you press on the top where the stem has broken off, it should be soft. The rind is coarse and the flesh is a bright orange.

The muskmelon is larger than the cantaloupe and more oblong. Its thick vein-like markings are columnar, resembling a pumpkin. The flesh is also bright orange with a lower water content but still sweet.

WATERMELON Watermelons should be heavy for their size, with a smooth surface, and firm but not hard. They are less aromatic than other melons; if they have a strong scent, they are probably overripe. Tap the watermelon and you should hear a hollow sound, indicating ripeness. The meat of the melon should be firm. To check this, pick the watermelon up and shake it. If you hear a sloshing sound, don't take it—the insides are mushy and overripe.

Yellow baby watermelons are extremely sweet with a firm, "chewy" texture. You'll find them only for two weeks at the beginning of September.

LABOR DAY MENU

Red New Potato Salad with Chopped Dill

Corn and Black Bean Salad with Diced Red Peppers

*Grilled Beefsteak Tomatoes and Pink Eggplant
   with Sliced Mozzarella*

Grilled Skirt Steak

Apple Tart

LABOR DAY WAS CREATED TO PAY TRIBUTE TO AMERICAN WORKERS and honor their contribution to our society and prosperity. While early celebrations focused on parades and speeches by labor leaders, officials, and educators, the way many people celebrate Labor Day today is with a barbecue to mark the end of the summer season. The markets are bursting with vegetables such as tomatoes, eggplant, and corn, which are at their peak. They make delicious accompaniments to a perfectly grilled steak, as in this menu.

Take the time on this holiday to think about where your food comes from and the labor that goes into bringing it to your table—trace it back from your preparation to the farmer who planted the crop or raised the cattle, and think about all the steps in between. Also remember to honor the work that you do throughout the year—not only the work you do to make a living and make a home for your family, but also the work that you do to maintain your recovery.

Red New Potato Salad with Chopped Dill

4 servings

12	red new potatoes, quartered
½	cup virgin olive oil
2	tablespoons white vinegar
1	tablespoon fresh lemon juice
2	tablespoons chopped fresh dill
	salt and black pepper

Bring a large pot of water to boil. Add the potatoes to the boiling water and cook about 12 minutes or until tender. Drain and let cool in a large bowl. (Warning: Do not run the cooked potatoes under cold water! It will make them gooey.)

When the potatoes are cool, add the olive oil, vinegar, lemon juice, and dill. Season with salt and pepper, and mix gently. Refrigerate until serving time.

Corn and Black Bean Salad with Diced Red Peppers

4 servings

Not only is this salad beautiful with the vibrant colors of summer, but it's also packed with nutritional value. Corn is loaded with vitamin C, potassium, and folic acid. It has plenty of fiber and makes a great protein source when combined with legumes, such as black beans.

1	cup dried black beans, soaked overnight
1	bay leaf
1	clove
1	tablespoon salt
2	ears of corn
¾	cup virgin olive oil
2	large red peppers, diced
1	medium red onion, sliced
½	cup chopped fresh cilantro
	juice of 1 lemon
¼	cup cider vinegar
	salt and black pepper to taste

Fill a large stockpot with water and bring to a boil. Drain the black beans and place in the stockpot; add the bay leaf, clove, and salt. Cook until tender (about 1 hour). Drain, let cool, and set aside.

Meanwhile, husk the corn and wipe clean. Run a small paring knife down the cob to remove the kernels. Heat 1 tablespoon olive oil and sauté the corn kernels for 4 to 6 minutes. Cook the corn just long enough to extract the sweetness from the kernels. Season with salt and pepper and let cool.

In a large bowl, combine the beans, corn, red peppers, onion, cilantro, and remaining olive oil. Add the lemon juice and vinegar, mix well, and season to taste. Refrigerate until ready to serve.

Grilled Beefsteak Tomatoes and Pink Eggplant with Sliced Mozzarella

4 servings

4 ripe beefsteak tomatoes
2 medium-size pink eggplants
1 pound fresh mozzarella
¼ cup virgin olive oil
   salt and black pepper to taste
2 tablespoons chopped basil

Slice the tomatoes, eggplant, and fresh mozzarella into rounds ¼ inch thick. Brush the tomatoes and eggplant with the olive oil and season with salt and pepper. Grill the tomatoes and eggplant 2 minutes on each side.

To assemble, stack a slice of eggplant, a slice of mozzarella, and a slice of tomato on a salad plate. Drizzle with the remaining olive oil and finish with the chopped basil.

Grilled Skirt Steak

4 servings

- ½ cup soy sauce
- ¼ cup Worcestershire sauce
- 1 sprig fresh rosemary, chopped
- 3 garlic cloves, chopped
- ¼ cup virgin olive oil
- 1½ pounds skirt steak, cut into 4 6-ounce pieces

Whisk together the soy sauce, Worcestershire sauce, rosemary, garlic, and olive oil. In a large pan, marinate the steak in the soy sauce mixture for 2 hours.

Steak is best cooked over high heat, so prepare a hot fire in your barbecue grill. The grill is ready when the coals are starting to turn gray. Brush the grate with olive oil and place the steaks on it. Cook 3 minutes, turn, and continue to cook until medium rare. Remove the steaks and slice into thin strips across the grain at a 45° angle.

Apple Tart

Makes three 10-inch tarts

This is just one perfect example of how to use a seasonal fruit at the right time in the right way. As a light dessert for an outdoor party or picnic around Labor Day, what could be better than an American apple tart? MacIntosh apples come to the market in early September.

Puff pastry makes a surprisingly quick, easy, and tasty base for apple tarts. It can be purchased fresh at most specialty stores or frozen in the grocery store. If you get frozen puff pastry, let it thaw in the refrigerator before you roll it out.

- 8 medium MacIntosh apples
- 1 pound puff pastry
- 1 cup sugar
- ½ teaspoon cinnamon

Roll the puff pastry to ½ inch thickness. Take a 10-inch cake circle and, using a pastry cutter or sharp knife, cut around the circle to make 3 10-inch tart shells. With a fork, pierce the dough so it won't puff up in the oven. Place the shells on a baking sheet and store in the refrigerator until you are ready to use them.

Preheat the oven to 350°.

Peel and core the apples, and slice ¼ inch thick. Remove the pastry from the refrigerator and place the apples on the shells in uniform layers.

Put the tarts into the preheated oven. Combine the sugar and cinnamon. After the tarts have been in the oven 15 minutes, liberally sprinkle cinnamon sugar on top of the apples. Continue baking approximately 15 minutes. With a spatula, lift each shell and make certain the puff pastry is crisp on the bottom. When crisp, remove from the oven, cut into fourths, and serve.

THOUGHTS ON RECOVERY

Cooking is like many other things in life: When you are willing to take a chance and end up with a different result from the one you planned, you have less pressure and more fun. Some of the best foods I have prepared in the kitchen were "mistakes." The only way to become a good cook is to give yourself time to gain experience, allowing yourself to be imperfect and to learn as you go. Your skills will develop over time. Always remember, there is another meal and another day.

Gandhi once said, "It is insignificant *what* we do, yet significant that we *do* it." With so many things I've done, I didn't know if they were the right thing to do at the time. But if I didn't take the action, I would have regretted what could have been, and that is the worst feeling of all. It's important to try, to take risks.

For example, when I first heard about my current job, I was on a retreat and a friend told me that Hazelden was looking for a chef. And I said I was not moving to Minnesota; it is too cold! And he said, "No, *right here in New York!*" I said, "I'm a restaurant chef." But I was unemployed and the rent was due, so I was willing to talk. It turned out to be the best decision I have made in recovery, other than asking my wife to marry me. It is funny, when you are humble, you are more willing to take a chance. It is something I learned about myself in recovery that lets me know that I'm human.

Autumn

Food fills your stomach,
but bread fills your soul.

Sweet and Spicy Spaghetti Squash

Chick-pea Casserole with Brown Rice and Steamed Kale

THANKSGIVING DINNER

Roast Turkey with Honey Glaze
Cranberry-Orange Relish
Broccoli and Spinach Casserole

Corn Bread and Sausage Dressing
Baked Sweet Potatoes
Pumpkin Cheesecake

My wife and I love to drive through the countryside in upstate New York at this time of year to watch the leaves turn color, sip hot apple cider, and eat fresh pumpkin bread. The markets are filled with produce that is not only delicious, but also decorative. You can display fresh produce at home, in a very natural way, simply arranging the different shapes of gourds and pumpkins and the myriad colors of Indian corn and whole corn stalks. Dried leaves and flowers also provide an endless array of texture and color.

The weather is cooler, so we break out our sweaters and sleep soundly under blankets. We go from the hot summer to the cool autumn, turning on the oven and baking bread.

Whenever I sit down to eat, whether at home or out, I always reach for the bread. It is the first thing I taste. Nothing makes me feel more taken care of than freshly baked bread. When you enter a home, the aroma of baking bread welcomes you in and helps you feel comfortable immediately. No matter how little you have, when you have fresh bread you always seem to have enough.

One of the first things I did at Hazelden New York was to begin making fresh bread daily. This immediately gave the dining room a more family-like atmosphere. The response from residents and staff was overwhelmingly positive. They were grateful that we took the time and care to make fresh bread for them. Bread offers comfort.

The Autumn Market

You turn around and summer is gone. You begin waiting for the first frost and the onset of winter. As you drive down the country roads, you see signs everywhere that say, "Pick your own apples." The farmers want to get their crops picked before the first frost arrives. It's the harvest season.

The markets are bursting with fresh produce: broccoli, brussels sprouts, cabbage, cauliflower, leeks, mushrooms, rutabagas, turnips, and winter squash.

BROCCOLI When purchasing broccoli, notice that the flowers should be compact and green, not yellow. The stems should be short in comparison with the head, and the stems should be tender and firm. A long, thick, woody stem indicates overmaturity. Broccoli comes into the market in late September and stays through the fall. Broccoli stores well in a plastic bag for up to one week. Make sure it does not frost in an overly cold refrigerator.

BRUSSELS SPROUTS Brussels sprouts are miniature cabbages, which originated in Belgium in the fourteenth century. Look for brussels sprouts that are small, very firm and compact, and rich in color. Yellow leaves indicate that they are past their prime. Brussels sprouts come to market in mid-autumn and are available through mid-winter. The best way to store them is in a covered container in the refrigerator, no more than a couple of days.

CABBAGE Cabbage can be green or red. Choose a cabbage that is firm, heavy for its size, with no discolored veins. Cabbage appears in the market in September and stays all through the fall. Remove its outer leaves and place it in an airtight container, and it can last up to one month in the lower part of the refrigerator.

When people think of cabbage, they think of its pungent flavor and strong aroma; but, when prepared properly, it is quite elegant. When preparing cabbage, remove the outer leaves, cut the head into quarters, and remove the core. One of my favorite ways of enjoying cabbage is by caramelizing onions, adding sliced cabbage, and cooking the mixture until tender, deglazing with cider vinegar and adding a little sugar.

Cabbage is a healthful food because it cleanses the colon and therefore enables nutrients to be absorbed more easily.

CAULIFLOWER When choosing cauliflower, make sure the curds are tight, the head is dense, and the leaves are crisp. The head should be a creamy white color. If the cauliflower has a strong cabbage smell, it is past its prime. This vegetable arrives in mid-September and stays through the fall.

Cauliflower lends itself to strong flavors. It mixes well in marinades and stews, or it can simply be steamed with cumin and chili powder.

LEEKS Leeks are in the onion family but are much sweeter and milder than yellow onions. They are usually used to enhance the flavor of soups, stews, and sauces. They make a great accompaniment to seafood. They are typically braised in chicken stock with a tablespoon of butter and a tablespoon of chopped herbs.

Leeks, you'll notice, are usually about two-thirds green and one-third white. Often, only the white part is used, making leeks very expensive to purchase. When picking out leeks at the market, look for the ones with the largest proportion of white to green.

To store leeks, cut off and discard the thick, darker green parts and store the rest in the bottom of the refrigerator up to two weeks.

RUTABAGAS AND TURNIPS Rutabagas are larger than turnips and have a yellow flesh and a more distinct flavor. Their skin is a buff color. For best flavor, their diameter should be no larger than four inches.

Turnips, on the other hand, have a white tip with a purple body and their flesh is white. They should be no more than two inches in diameter. Turnips have a slightly spicy flavor and a crisp texture. They work well in stews and soups. They can often be used in place of potatoes.

Both rutabagas and turnips should be firm with no blemishes. A definite sign of freshness is the presence of their top leaves intact. They store very well with their tops removed and placed in an airtight container in the bottom of the refrigerator. Turnips can be stored in this way up to two weeks and rutabagas up to one month. They retain their nutritional value longer than most vegetables.

Rutabagas can be puréed or used in soups. One of the ways I use rutabagas is as follows: Peel and slice the rutabaga. Partially cook the slices in salted boiling water, drain, and set aside. Caramelize onions; add rehydrated raisins, apricots, figs; stir in some honey and a pinch of cardamom. Toss with the rutabagas and bake in an oiled casserole dish until tender.

One of the ways I like to use turnips is with a pork roast, making a gravy with the drippings and the roasted turnips.

WINTER SQUASH There are many varieties of winter squash; some of the most popular include acorn, butternut, hubbard, and spaghetti. *Acorn squash* is sweet and delicate. It is best cooked whole and stuffed and served with poultry. *Butternut squash* flesh is more mealy and starchy and is better mashed or puréed. *Hubbard squash* flesh is a bright orange, with a sweet, earthy flavor, great in soups. *Spaghetti squash* is stringy like spaghetti; it is high in fiber and delicious tossed in pasta.

At the market, select squash that are heavy for their size; this will ensure more flesh on the inside. Make sure there are no cracks or soft spots. You can store squash at room temperature up to three months.

To cook winter squash, I like to cut the squash lengthwise, scoop out the seeds, rub the cut flesh with olive oil, and sprinkle it with salt. I place the squash cut side down on a baking sheet and roast at 400 degrees until tender, about 45 minutes. Roasting in the dry heat brings out the natural sweetness of the squash.

BREAD MAKING

Quick Breads
Banana Bread
Corn Bread
Pumpkin Bread

Yeast Breads
Italian Bread
Bacon-Onion Flat Bread
Challah
Apple-Raisin Pan Bread
Soft Rolls
Whole Wheat Rolls
Garlic Knots
Basil-Onion Rolls

WHEN I THINK OF BREAD, I think of my mother, soft and warm. Preparing and baking fresh bread is an expression of love—of self and of those around us—shown through the action. Food fills your stomach, but bread fills your soul. Bread is the first and the last thing I eat during a meal; it is the perfect accompaniment to any dish on any occasion. With bread, you take the most basic ingredients and make the staff of life.

*Gino and his wife, Laurie, (center left) share a meal at home
with their close friends Jade (left) and Mike (right).*

Banana Bread

Makes 2 loaves

6	cups pastry flour
4	tablespoons baking powder
½	teaspoon salt
1	teaspoon baking soda
1	pound (4 sticks) soft butter
2	cups sugar
5	eggs
4	cups mashed ripe bananas (about 4)
1	cup chopped walnuts

Preheat the oven to 350°. Butter and flour 2 loaf pans.

Sift the pastry flour, baking powder, salt, and baking soda into a bowl.

In a mixing bowl, beat together the butter and sugar. Cream together until smooth. (I use a paddle attachment on my stand mixer, but you could use a hand mixer or beat by hand as well.)

Add 1 cup of the dry ingredients to the butter mixture. Lightly beat the eggs in a small bowl. Add the eggs in 3 stages, alternating with adding 1 cup of the dry ingredients. Make sure the eggs are incorporated before you add more of the dry ingredients (this will ensure that your batter will not separate). After all the eggs are mixed in, add the rest of the dry ingredients. Mix *only* until the wet and dry ingredients are blended; do not overmix.

Add the bananas and walnuts. Mix until they are evenly distributed throughout the batter.

Divide the batter evenly between the loaf pans and bake about 45 minutes, or until a toothpick inserted in the center comes out clean.

Turn the bread out onto a baking rack, letting air circulate around the bread so that it cools more quickly.

Corn Bread

Makes 2 loaves

I like to use whole milk in this recipe. The extra milkfat makes the bread richer, with a softer texture than if you used skim milk.

- 2 cups pastry flour
- 3 cups cornmeal
- 4 tablespoons baking powder
- ½ teaspoon salt
- ½ pound (2 sticks) butter, softened
- 1 cup sugar
- 4 large eggs
- 2 cups whole milk
- 1½ cups whole frozen corn kernels

Set a rack in the middle of the oven and preheat to 350°.

In a mixing bowl, sift together the pastry flour, cornmeal, baking powder, and salt.

In another bowl, beat together the butter and sugar. Cream together until smooth. (I use a paddle attachment on my stand mixer, but you could use a hand mixer or beat by hand as well.)

Add 1 cup of the dry ingredients to the butter mixture. Whisk the eggs and milk together in a small bowl. Add the eggs in 3 stages, alternating with adding 1 cup of the dry ingredients. Make sure the eggs are incorporated before you add more of the dry ingredients (this will ensure that your batter will not separate). After all the eggs are mixed in, add the rest of the dry ingredients. Mix only until the wet and dry ingredients are blended; do not overmix.

Add the whole corn kernels. Mix until they are evenly distributed throughout the batter.

Divide the batter evenly between 2 buttered loaf pans.

Bake 45 minutes or until a toothpick inserted in the center of the bread comes out dry. Turn the bread out onto a baking rack, letting air circulate, to cool more quickly.

Pumpkin Bread

Makes 2 loaves

¾ pound (3 sticks) soft butter
1½ cups sugar
5 cups pastry flour
2 tablespoons baking powder
½ teaspoon salt
½ teaspoon baking soda
   pinch nutmeg
⅛ teaspoon cinnamon
4 large eggs
1 pound canned pumpkin purée
¾ cup chopped walnuts

Set a rack in the middle of the oven and preheat to 350°.

In a mixing bowl, beat together the butter and sugar. Cream together until smooth. (I use a paddle attachment on my stand mixer, but you could use a hand mixer or beat by hand as well.)

In a separate bowl, sift together the pastry flour, baking powder, salt, soda, nutmeg, and cinnamon.

Add 1 cup of the dry ingredients to the butter mixture. Lightly beat the eggs in a small bowl. Add the eggs in 3 stages, alternating with adding 1 cup of the dry ingredients. Make sure the eggs are incorporated before you add more of the dry ingredients (this will ensure that your batter will not separate). After all the eggs are mixed in, add the rest of the dry ingredients. Mix only until the wet and dry ingredients are blended; do not overmix.

Add the pumpkin purée and walnuts and mix until they are evenly distributed throughout the batter.

Divide the batter evenly between 2 buttered loaf pans, and bake 45 minutes or until a toothpick inserted in the center of the bread comes out dry.

Turn the baked bread out onto a baking rack, letting air circulate, to cool more quickly.

Italian Bread

Makes 4 loaves

 2 tablespoons (2 envelopes) dry yeast
1¾ cups water
 3 tablespoons virgin olive oil
 1 tablespoon granulated sugar
 1 tablespoon salt
 3 cups bread flour
 2 cups durum flour
    extra durum flour for dusting
 ½ cup beaten egg whites (about 3 egg whites)
 ½ cup sesame seeds

Combine the yeast and water in the bowl of a stand mixer and let sit 10 minutes. Add the olive oil, sugar, and salt and ferment another 10 minutes.

Sift the bread flour and durum flour together and add to the liquid. Using the dough hook attachment, mix at low speed for 10 minutes. Dust the sides of the bowl with the extra flour from time to time so the dough doesn't stick.

Oil a large mixing bowl and transfer the dough to the bowl, turning the dough in the bowl so the top is oiled. Cover with plastic wrap and let proof (rise) 1 hour or until doubled in size.

Dust the work area and grease a large baking sheet. Transfer the dough to your work surface and knead lightly. Divide the dough into 4 equal pieces and knead into 4 separate balls. Then roll into 12-inch-long loaves. Place on your greased sheet pan. With a sharp knife, make 2 diagonal slits on each loaf, each slit about 4 inches in length. Let proof another hour.

Place quarry tile on a sheet pan in the oven (or use a baking stone) and preheat to 400° at least 45 minutes. The stones should be very hot. Brush the loaves with the beaten egg whites. Slide the loaves directly onto the hot tile. Bake 15 minutes. Remove the loaves from the oven and brush quickly with the egg whites again, and sprinkle with the sesame seeds. Spray the sides of the oven with water to develop steam, which helps create a crisp crust, and then bake another 15 minutes.

Remove from the oven, place on a baking rack, and let cool.

Bacon-Onion Flat Bread

Makes 8 flat breads

3	tablespoons (3 envelopes) dry yeast
1½	cups lukewarm water
½	cup shortening
2	cups chopped onions
2	cups chopped bacon or pancetta
5	cups bread flour, sifted
2	egg whites
1	tablespoon sugar
1	tablespoon salt

Mix the yeast and water and let ferment 10 minutes.

In the meantime, heat 1 teaspoon shortening and sauté the onions until they are translucent. Sauté the bacon over low heat until crisp. Drain the fat and let cool.

Add the sugar, salt, shortening, onions, and bacon to the yeast and water. Ferment another 10 minutes.

Combine all the ingredients except the egg whites in a mixing bowl. Mix with a dough hook at low speed 10 minutes, dusting with flour to make sure the dough does not stick to the bowl. Place in a greased stainless steel bowl, cover with plastic wrap, and let proof (rise) about 1 hour until double in size.

Turn out onto a floured work area, divide into 8 pieces, knead each into a ball, and roll each into a flat log about 12 inches long, 4 inches wide and ¼ inch thick. Make several slits with a sharp knife 2 inches apart across each log. The slit should not go all the way across, leaving about ½-inch margin on each side. Place on a greased baking sheet and let rise 30 minutes.

Preheat the oven to 400°.

Bake 10 minutes, brush with the egg whites, and bake another 10 minutes to form a hard crust.

Remove from the oven, place on a baking rack, and let cool. Serve whole, letting your guests tear off their own pieces, making the breaking of bread a communal experience!

Challah

Makes 2 loaves

Challah is a special part of Jewish meals, so special that it is not called bread, it is called challah. There are many stories in Jewish culture about challah and its meaning. It is used at every important event from the Friday night Sabbath meal to weddings to bar mitzvahs. Challah is also used during the week, elevating the simplest meal to a special occasion.

1¾	cup lukewarm water (about 110°)
3	tablespoons (3 envelopes) dry yeast
4	egg yolks
½	tablespoon salt
2	tablespoons sugar
2	tablespoons vegetable oil
2	tablespoons honey
5	cups bread flour, sifted
	extra bread flour for dusting
	egg wash: 2 eggs lightly beaten with 2 tablespoons water

Combine the water and yeast in the mixing bowl of a stand mixer and let ferment 10 minutes. Add the egg yolks, salt, sugar, vegetable oil, and honey to the yeast and water and let ferment another 10 minutes.

Add the flour to the liquid and mix with a dough hook 10 minutes at low speed. Dust with flour as the dough is mixing, so the dough doesn't stick to the sides of the mixing bowl. From time to time, stop the mixer to push the dough down from the hook (as it is mixing it winds up, sticking to and climbing up the hook).

Place the dough in a large oiled bowl. Brush the top of the dough with vegetable oil and cover with plastic wrap. Let proof (rise) 1 hour or until the dough doubles in size.

Turn the dough out onto a floured work area. With a dough scraper, cut the dough in half. Divide each half into 3 equal parts and form 6 dough balls. Place 1 dough ball at a time on a floured surface and roll with palms while pressing down, forming a 12-inch cylinder.

To braid the challah, pinch the ends of 3 cylinders together. Place the left piece over the middle piece (so now *it* becomes the middle piece). Next, place the right piece over the middle piece. Continue braiding until you come to the end. Pinch the ends together and turn the pinched parts under the loaf. Place on a greased baking sheet and cover with oiled plastic wrap. Let proof again until double in size.

When the loaves are almost doubled, preheat the oven to 400° and prepare the egg wash. Bake the challahs 20 minutes; then remove and brush the tops and sides with the egg wash. Lower the oven temperature to 350° and bake another 20 minutes or until golden brown.

Transfer to a rack to cool.

Apple-Raisin Pan Bread

Makes 2 loaves

2	tablespoons (2 envelopes) dry yeast
2	cups lukewarm water
½	cup light brown sugar
1	tablespoon salt
4	whole eggs
2	tablespoons soft butter
½	teaspoon cardamom
½	teaspoon mace
2	teaspoons cinnamon
5½	cups bread flour
	extra bread flour for dusting
2	Granny Smith apples, peeled, cored, and diced
½	cup raisins
½	cup roughly chopped walnuts
½	cup granulated sugar
	egg wash: 2 eggs lightly beaten with 2 tablespoons water

In the work bowl of a stand mixer, combine the yeast and water and let stand for 10 minutes. Add the brown sugar, salt, eggs, butter, cardamom, mace, and 1 teaspoon of the cinnamon. Blend together and ferment another 10 minutes.

Sift the flour and add to the yeast mixture. Mix 5 minutes with a dough hook at low speed. Dust with extra flour from time to time, making sure the dough does not stick to the sides of the bowl.

Transfer the dough to a large oiled bowl. Cover with plastic wrap and let proof (rise) 1 hour or until double in size.

While the dough is rising, rehydrate the raisins 5 minutes in enough hot water to cover them. Drain, squeeze out excess water, and pat dry.

Preheat the oven to 400° and roast the walnuts on a baking sheet about 5 minutes, until they are lightly browned and fragrant. Reserve 2 tablespoons of the walnuts for topping.

In a small bowl, mix the raisins, roasted walnuts, apples, granulated sugar, and remaining 1 teaspoon of cinnamon. Set aside.

Oil two 12-inch loaf pans and dust a work surface with flour. Turn the dough out onto the floured work area. Divide the dough into 2 equal pieces. Knead by hand for 2 minutes and roll each piece into a rectangle. Spread the fruit filling over the dough. Fold the dough into thirds, like a business letter, and then fold in half. Roll into cylinders making two 12-inch loaves.

Bake 15 minutes. Remove from the oven, brush quickly with the egg wash, and sprinkle with the reserved chopped walnuts. Bake another 20 minutes, remove from the oven, and cool 10 minutes. Unmold on a baking rack and cool another 20 minutes. Slice and serve warm.

Soft Rolls

Makes 12 rolls

These sweet, tender rolls make a wonderful everyday roll that complements a wide variety of meals. Increased shortening is what makes the roll soft.

3	tablespoons (3 envelopes) dry yeast
1½	cups lukewarm water
2	teaspoons salt
½	cup sugar
1½	cups shortening, melted (reserve 2 tablespoons)
5½	cups bread flour (reserve ½ cup for dusting)
	egg wash: 2 eggs lightly beaten with 2 tablespoons water
1	tablespoon poppy seeds
1	tablespoon sesame seeds

Combine the yeast and water in the bowl of your stand mixer and let ferment 10 minutes. Add the salt, sugar, and shortening to the yeast and water, and let ferment another 10 minutes.

Sift the flour; then add to the liquid. Mix 10 minutes with a dough hook on a low speed.

Transfer the dough to an oiled bowl. Brush the top of the dough with 2 tablespoons of melted shortening and cover with plastic wrap. Let proof (rise) 1 hour or until the dough doubles in size.

Dust a work area with flour. Turn the dough out onto the floured work area. Divide the dough in half. Roll each half into a thick cylinder; slice each cylinder into 6 parts to form 12 pieces of dough. To shape the rolls, cup your hand over a piece of dough and gently press into the work surface. With a circular motion, work the dough with your palm into a smooth, round ball. Place on a greased sheet pan and let rest until almost double in size, about 1 hour.

Preheat the oven to 400°.

Bake 10 minutes; then brush with the egg wash. Lower the oven temperature to 350°. Sprinkle the poppy seeds on half the rolls and the sesame seeds on the other half. Bake another 10 minutes. When done, remove the rolls from the oven and place on a baking rack to cool.

Whole Wheat Rolls

Makes 12 rolls

2   tablespoons (2 envelopes) dry yeast
2   cups lukewarm water
½   cup honey
2   tablespoons salt
2   tablespoons sugar
½   cup powdered buttermilk
4   eggs
½   cup (1 stick) soft butter
3   cups bread flour
2   cups whole wheat flour
    extra whole wheat flour for dusting
    egg wash: 2 eggs lightly beaten with 2 tablespoons water

Dissolve the yeast in the water and let stand 10 minutes. Add the honey, salt, sugar, powdered buttermilk, eggs, and butter, and blend together. Ferment another 10 minutes.

Sift the bread flour and whole wheat flour together and add to the yeast mixture. With a dough hook, mix 7 minutes at low speed. Dust the bowl with flour from time to time as you are mixing, making sure the dough does not stick to the sides of the bowl. Transfer the dough to a large oiled bowl. Cover with plastic wrap and let proof (rise) 1 hour or until double in size.

Dust a work area with whole wheat flour and turn the dough out onto it. Divide into 24 equal pieces. Roll into balls and place on a greased baking sheet. With a sharp knife, make a decorative slit in the middle of each roll and let proof (rise) another hour.

While the rolls are rising preheat the oven to 400° for 45 minutes. Bake the rolls 10 minutes. Remove from the oven and brush quickly with the egg wash and bake another 10 minutes. When done, remove from the oven and place on a baking rack. Cool 20 minutes and serve warm.

Garlic Knots

Makes 24 rolls

2 tablespoons (2 envelopes) dry yeast

2 cups lukewarm water

1 tablespoon salt

1 tablespoon sugar

2 tablespoons virgin olive oil

2 tablespoons honey

7 cups bread flour

extra bread flour for dusting

TOPPING

4 garlic cloves, thinly sliced

1½ cups virgin olive oil

¼ cup grated Parmesan cheese

Combine the yeast and water in the bowl of your stand mixer and let ferment 10 minutes. Add the salt, sugar, oil, and honey to the yeast and water and let ferment another 10 minutes.

Sift the flour; then add it to the liquid. Using the dough hook, mix for 10 minutes at second speed. Dust from time to time with flour so the dough does not stick to the sides of the bowl.

Turn the dough out into a large oiled bowl. Brush the top of the dough with oil and cover with plastic wrap. Let proof (rise) 1 hour or until the dough doubles in size.

Grease 2 large baking sheets and dust your work area with flour. Turn the dough out onto the floured surface. With a dough scraper, cut the dough into 24 equal pieces (about 2 ounces each, a little bigger than a golf ball) and form balls. Place 1 dough ball at a time on the floured surface and roll with your palms while pressing down, forming 4-inch-long cylinders (like cigars). Tie each piece in a knot and place on the baking sheet.

Let the rolls proof again until double in size, about an hour. When the rolls are almost double, preheat the oven to 400°.

Bake the rolls 10 minutes. Meanwhile, prepare the topping: Heat the oil and simmer the garlic until it is golden. Add the Parmesan cheese, mix, and brush onto the rolls. Bake the rolls another 10 minutes or until golden brown. Cool the rolls on a rack.

Basil-Onion Rolls

Makes 12 rolls

2	tablespoons (2 envelopes) dry yeast
1¾	cups lukewarm water
4	tablespoons virgin olive oil
½	onion, diced
2	tablespoons salt
1	tablespoon black pepper
2	tablespoons sugar
2	tablespoons dried basil
5	cups bread flour
½	cup cornmeal for dusting

Dissolve the yeast in water and let stand 10 minutes.

Meanwhile, heat the oil and sauté the onion until translucent. Add the salt, pepper, sugar, and basil. Cool to room temperature, add to the yeast mixture, and let ferment 10 minutes.

Sift the bread flour and add to the yeast mixture. Mix 10 minutes at low speed with a dough hook. From time to time, dust the sides of the bowl with a handful of bread flour so the dough does not stick to the sides. Place the dough in a greased bowl, cover with plastic wrap, and let proof (rise) 1 hour or until double in size.

Dust your work surface and a large baking sheet with cornmeal. Transfer the dough to your work area and divide the dough into 12 equal pieces. Roll the pieces of dough between your hand and the work surface, stretching the dough "down" so the balls of dough are tight. Place the finished rolls on your dusted baking sheet, spray lightly with water, and dust the tops with cornmeal. Let proof 1 hour or until double in size.

While the dough is proofing, place quarry tile on a baking sheet in the oven and preheat to 400° for 45 minutes.

Place the raised rolls directly on the hot quarry tile and bake 20 minutes. Remove 1 roll from the oven and tap the bottom. If it sounds hollow, it is ready. Remove all the rolls from the oven and place on a baking rack to cool.

VEGETARIAN DISHES

Stuffed Acorn Squash

Butternut Squash Purée

Chick-pea Casserole

Eggplant Parmesan

Hubbard Squash Soup

Sweet and Spicy Spaghetti Squash

OVER THE LAST FEW YEARS, I have become much more aware of the nutritional makeup of the food I cook and eat. To be healthy, we need balance in all parts of our lives, including our diet. Just as we nourish our minds with a variety of experiences, we need to nourish our bodies with a variety of foods.

We're beginning to understand the importance of eating a lighter, more varied diet. One of the best ways to do that is to dine on several meatless meals each week. This keeps down the intake of animal fat, which is high in calories and difficult to digest, and increases the amount of complex carbohydrates in the diet. Combining beans and grains offers complete proteins and more fiber, which in turn aids digestion and nutrient absorption. Vegetarian cooking is also economical, especially when you take advantage of fresh, locally grown produce.

The recipes I've included here for you to sample focus on several simple ways to prepare some of the most abundant and nutritious autumn vegetables.

Stuffed Acorn Squash

6 servings

This is a hearty dish on its own, or great to serve with your holiday turkey.

6 acorn squash, 6 inches in diameter
2 tablespoons virgin olive oil
1 teaspoon salt
½ teaspoon cardamom

STUFFING
4 cups frozen chopped spinach (about 3 boxes), thawed
1 tablespoon virgin olive oil
1 onion, finely chopped
2 garlic cloves, finely chopped
2 cups heavy cream
1 teaspoon salt
½ teaspoon pepper
⅛ teaspoon cardamom

Preheat the oven to 350°. Cut the tops off the squash and reserve. Spoon out the seeds, rub with the olive oil, and sprinkle with the salt and cardamom. Arrange the cut side up in a large roasting pan filled with ½ inch water. Bake 20 minutes.

Meanwhile, prepare the stuffing. Drain the spinach and squeeze out most of the liquid. Heat the oil and sauté the onion and garlic until slightly golden. Add the heavy cream, salt, pepper, and cardamom. Simmer until reduced by half. Add the spinach and simmer another 5 to 6 minutes.

Fill the acorn squash with the creamed spinach, replace the reserved tops, and bake another 20 minutes.

Butternut Squash Purée

4 to 6 servings

> 2 butternut squash
> 3 tablespoons virgin olive oil
> 1 tablespoon salt
> 2 large white potatoes, peeled and diced
> 1 onion, finely chopped
> 1 cup milk
> 1   teaspoon salt
> ½ teaspoon black pepper
> ⅛ teaspoon freshly grated nutmeg

Preheat the oven to 400°. Cut the squash lengthwise, scoop out the seeds, rub the flesh with 1 tablespoon of the olive oil, and sprinkle with salt. Place the cut side down in a roasting pan, and roast until tender (about 45 minutes).

While the squash is in the oven, cook the potatoes in boiling salted water 6 to 8 minutes until tender. Drain and purée in a food processor or mash by hand.

Remove the squash from the oven. When cool enough to handle, scoop out the flesh and purée in a food processor (or mash by hand like the potatoes).

Heat the remaining olive oil in a large sauté pan and sauté the onion until golden. Add the pureed squash and potatoes and simmer 3 to 4 minutes. Stir constantly with a wooden spoon (see note) and add the milk. Continue simmering 8 to 10 minutes. Serve in a deep bowl and garnish with freshly grated nutmeg.

NOTE: A wooden spoon is used because a metal spoon scraping a metal pot can release particles, resulting in oxidation and discoloration of food.

Chick-pea Casserole

4 servings

Served with brown rice and steamed kale or any green leafy vegetable, this makes a perfect vegetarian meal, low in fat and high in protein, with the combination of legumes and grain. By substituting seasonal vegetables, you can prepare this dish year round.

1 cup dried chick peas, soaked overnight
1 tablespoon salt
1 bay leaf
1 clove
1 hubbard squash, roasted and diced
   (see the roasting method for squash on page 135)
4 potatoes, diced
1 carrot, diced
1 celery root (if you can't find celery root, use 2 celery stalks), diced
4 tablespoons virgin olive oil
1 onion, chopped
2 garlic cloves, chopped
1 cup freshly chopped dill (½ to 1 bunch)
4 tomatoes, diced
1 cup vegetable stock
   salt and black pepper to taste
1 cup grated mozzarella cheese

Place the chick-peas in a large stockpot and completely cover with water. Bring the water to a boil; then turn down the heat and add the salt, bay leaf, and clove. Simmer about 1 hour or until tender. Drain and set aside.

While the chick-peas are simmering, prepare the hubbard squash.

Boil the potatoes in a stockpot of water until they are about two-thirds done (about 6 minutes). Drain and set aside.

Steam the carrot and celery root for 3 minutes and set aside.

Heat 2 tablespoons olive oil in a large sauté pan and sauté the onion and garlic over medium heat until golden. Add the steamed carrots and celery root and continue cooking 3 to 4 minutes. Add the chick-peas and chopped dill, and a pinch of salt, which helps to bring out the flavor. Continue cooking 6 to 8 minutes.

Preheat the oven to 400°.

Add the tomatoes, hubbard squash, and potatoes and cook another 4 minutes. When stirring, try not to break up the potatoes and squash. Add the stock and adjust the seasoning. Cook another 5 minutes and finish with the rest of the olive oil.

Spoon the casserole into an oiled ovenproof dish, cover with the grated mozzarella cheese, and bake until golden.

Eggplant Parmesan

6 servings

This classic Italian dish is one of the most popular eggplant dishes in the United States. Making the tomato sauce from scratch adds extra time and cooking effort, but the aroma and the result are wonderful. It's not a light dish by any means, with the fried eggplant and ricotta cheese filling, but it is warm and comforting food that evokes the abundance of autumn.

TOMATO SAUCE
2   tablespoons virgin olive oil
1   onion, diced
2   garlic cloves, chopped
8   cups whole canned tomatoes, pureed in food processor
1   bay leaf
1   tablespoon dried basil
1   teaspoon dried oregano
½   teaspoon dried thyme
1   tablespoon salt
1   teaspoon black pepper

Preheat the oven to 350°. In a large ovenproof sauté pan, heat the olive oil and sauté the onion and garlic until they begin to turn golden. Add the tomatoes and the rest of the seasonings, bring to a boil, and then bake about 1 hour. The dry heat from the oven helps sweeten the sauce without the need for added sugar. When finished, let cool and set aside.

EGGPLANT

3   medium eggplants, peeled and sliced lengthwise ⅛ inch thick
6   eggs
1   tablespoon dried basil
1   teaspoon salt
1   teaspoon black pepper
4   cups dry breadcrumbs
2   cups Parmesan cheese
1   tablespoon chopped fresh parsley
    olive oil for frying

Place the eggplant slices in a colander and sprinkle with salt. Place 2 or 3 dinner plates on top of the eggplant slices to squeeze the bitter juices out. Let stand 2 or 3 hours.

In a small bowl, beat the eggs, basil, salt, and pepper. In another bowl, blend the breadcrumbs, Parmesan cheese, and parsley.

Bread the eggplant: Dip each slice of eggplant into the egg mixture, then the breadcrumbs, making sure the entire slice is coated. Place the slices on a platter and get ready to fry.

Fill bottom of a large skillet with olive oil (about ⅛ inch deep) and turn heat to medium. Fry the eggplant slices about 3 minutes, until they are golden on both sides and soft on the inside. You will need to do this in several batches. As the slices are finished, drain on absorbent paper towels to soak up the excess oil. Set aside.

FILLING

4   cups ricotta cheese
1   egg
2   teaspoons salt
½   teaspoon black pepper
1   teaspoon dried oregano
4   cups shredded mozzarella cheese
1   cup grated Parmesan cheese

In a mixing bowl, blend the ricotta cheese, egg, salt, pepper, and oregano. Set aside until you are ready to assemble the dish. In another bowl, blend the mozzarella and Parmesan cheese. Preheat oven to 350°.

Assemble the dish: Select a baking pan with 4-inch sides, and line the bottom with some of the tomato sauce. Next, place a layer of eggplant and spread half the ricotta filling on top. Drizzle with some tomato sauce. Place another layer of eggplant, spread the remaining ricotta filling on top, followed by a drizzling of tomato sauce. Place a third and final layer of eggplant. Spread the remaining tomato sauce on top, cover with the cheese mixture, and cover with aluminum foil.

Bake 45 minutes. Remove the aluminum foil and bake another 15 minutes, so the cheese becomes golden. Remove from the oven, let rest 20 minutes, and then cut into 4-inch squares. Place on a platter, garnish with fresh chopped parsley, and serve with pasta and garlic knots (see page 148) for a true Italian vegetarian special!

Hubbard Squash Soup

4 servings

1	tablespoon virgin olive oil
1	onion, finely diced
2	garlic cloves, finely diced
1	quart vegetable broth or water
4	cups hubbard squash, puréed (about 1 medium squash)
1	teaspoon salt
½	teaspoon black pepper
⅛	teaspoon cinnamon
⅛	teaspoon mace
1	cup heavy cream
½	cup chopped scallion

Heat the olive oil and sauté the onion and garlic until golden. Add the broth and simmer 15 minutes. Add the squash and the salt, pepper, cinnamon, and mace, and simmer for another 15 minutes. Add the heavy cream, and continue to simmer 5 to 6 minutes until heated through. Serve garnished with chopped scallion.

Sweet and Spicy Spaghetti Squash

4 servings

> 1 spaghetti squash
> 1 pound dried spaghetti
> ½ cup virgin olive oil
> 1 onion, thinly sliced
> 2 garlic cloves, thinly sliced
> 1 tablespoon dark brown sugar
> 2 fresh tomatoes, diced
> 2 small hot Italian peppers, diced
> 4 sprigs Italian parsley

Preheat the oven to 400°. Pierce the spaghetti squash shell all around with a fork. Rub with olive oil and bake whole 40 minutes or until tender. Let cool, cut in half lengthwise, and spoon the seeds out. Run a fork through the flesh, removing the flesh in spaghetti-like strands.

Bring a large pot of salted water to a rapid boil and add the dried spaghetti. Cook until al dente (slightly firm), about 8 minutes.

Heat ¼ cup olive oil in a large skillet and sauté the onion and garlic until golden. Add the brown sugar and dissolve over low heat. Add the diced tomatoes and chili peppers, and simmer 4 to 6 minutes. Add the spaghetti squash and simmer another 4 to 6 minutes. Add the cooked pasta and toss together. Separate into 4 portions and drizzle the remaining olive oil over the top. Garnish with the Italian parsley.

WORLD SERIES MENU

Cream of Tomato Soup

Honey-glazed Chicken with Mushrooms and Leeks

Braised Broccoli Rabe with Onions and Garlic

Olive Bread

Pecan Pie

IN 1996, THE YANKEES WON THE WORLD SERIES. I had been waiting for that since 1977. To me, the Yankees that year seemed like a team of destiny. They were true champions, playing great and taking advantage of the breaks they were given with their willingness to work hard to succeed.

I went to every home game during the playoffs. My brother-in-law Neal, my friend Rich, his son, and I slept out overnight on three separate occasions for tickets. Some of my friends thought I was crazy, but I didn't care. It was a lot of fun, playing touch football, talking through the night, and sharing our food. Laurie would stop by and drop off hot soup and sandwiches. All around us, people were drinking, but we felt no need to join in. It seemed unnecessary—all we needed was each other's company and healthy sustenance. There was a total eclipse of the moon the first night we camped out. I felt as if I was somewhere in the country, but I was in the Bronx!

When the games began, we came early and stayed late—arriving at the park for batting practice, celebrating after the game. When the Yankees were away, we would go over to each other's home and celebrate just like everyone else, except we were doing it sober and feeling good about it. This World Series menu is one I developed to celebrate my team and the sense of community and togetherness and joy that their victory brought about.

Cream of Tomato Soup

6 servings

I peel and seed the tomatoes for this soup because the skin can sometimes add bitterness, and the texture of the finished soup is so much creamier without seeds and bits of skin. Using heavy cream is also important. The extra fat gives the soup a velvety texture and cuts the acidity of the tomatoes so the cream won't curdle in the soup. If you want to make a lower fat version, you can replace the heavy cream with evaporated skim milk thickened with a little stock and cornstarch.

10 whole tomatoes, peeled, seeded, and chopped coarsely (see note)
 1 tablespoon virgin olive oil
 2 whole onions, thinly sliced
 4 garlic cloves, thinly sliced
 1 cup tomato purée
 1 quart chicken stock or vegetable stock
 1 cup heavy cream
 1 tablespoon salt
 1 teaspoon black pepper
 2 tablespoons chopped dill

Heat the olive oil in a large stockpot and sauté the onions and garlic until golden. Add the fresh tomatoes and purée and continue cooking 6 to 8 minutes at medium heat. Add the chicken stock and simmer 30 minutes. Strain through a fine-mesh sieve to separate the broth from the vegetables. Save the broth and puree the vegetables in a food processor. Combine the broth with the pureed vegetables, add the cream, salt, and pepper, and continue cooking another 10 minutes. Garnish with chopped dill and serve hot.

NOTE: To peel and seed tomatoes, cut an X on the bottom of each tomato, place in a large pot of boiling water, and boil 3 minutes. Remove from the water and plunge into ice water. When the tomatoes are cool, peel away the skin. Slice in half and squeeze out the seeds.

Honey-glazed Chicken with Mushrooms and Leeks

4 to 6 servings

2   2½-pound chickens, tied (see below)
1   tablespoon salt

GLAZE
1   cup honey
1   cup soy sauce
1   tablespoon Chinese chili oil
1   tablespoon Dijon mustard
1   cup cider vinegar

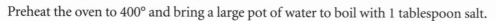

4   cups button mushrooms (about two 10-ounce packages)
4   cups leeks (white part only), sliced
1   quart chicken stock
2   tablespoons salt
1   sprig thyme (about 1 teaspoon)
1   bay leaf

Preheat the oven to 400° and bring a large pot of water to boil with 1 tablespoon salt.

Prepare the chicken: To tie the chickens, cut a piece of butcher's twine (purchase at a hardware store or from your local butcher) long enough to fit twice around the diameter of the bird. Position the chickens so that the drumsticks face up. Place the twine underneath the ends of the drumsticks. Make sure the twine is of equal length on either side of the bird. Cross the ends of the twine, making an X, pull the ends of the twine down toward the neck and pull twine around the body, catching the wing underneath the twine. Wrap the twine around the backbone and neck opening. Tie the two ends with a secure knot.

Place the chickens in the boiling water and leave in for 5 minutes. This will render some of the fat from the birds, and they will be crisper and less fatty when roasted. Remove from the water and pat dry.

Prepare the glaze: With a wire whisk, combine the honey, soy sauce, chili oil, mustard, and vinegar. Simmer over medium heat 20 to 30 minutes until reduced to a syrup-like consistency.

Place the chickens on a roasting rack in a large roasting pan, brush with glaze, and roast 20 minutes. Brush with glaze again, turn the heat down to 350°, and roast another 20 minutes.

Add the mushrooms, leeks, and chicken stock to the roasting pan. Brush the chickens with glaze once again and roast another 20 minutes, letting the natural juices drip into the chicken stock.

Remove the chickens from the oven and set aside to cool. Pour all the drippings and vegetables into a large heavy saucepan. Reduce the liquid by half. Cut the cooked chicken into quarters.

Place the quartered chicken in the saucepan with the drippings, add the salt, thyme, and bay leaf, and cook to heat all the way through. Remove the chicken and place on a serving platter. Pour the liquid with the mushrooms and leeks over the chicken and serve immediately. If you have any glaze left over, drizzle over the platter for added flavor.

Braised Broccoli Rabe with Onions and Garlic

6 servings

Growing up, I remember all the excitement when broccoli rabe would make its way to the table in early fall. My grandparents were so excited, but to me it was just another bitter vegetable. Now, I'm just as excited as they were. A variety of taste and textures is what makes a meal special. Tender and sweet greens are not always available. It is like life—you make the most of what you have at the time.

Related to the turnip, broccoli rabe is an Italian green bitter vegetable loaded with folic acid, B vitamins, and minerals that help reduce stress, which is important in early recovery. It arrives at the market in early fall and remains throughout winter. It has a distinct robust flavor and can be used as an accompaniment to pasta and sauces or as a vegetable on its own.

The arrival of broccoli rabe means another season, and as I get older I can appreciate the changes. I am grateful that I am still alive and can partake of life, the bitter and the sweet.

3 heads broccoli rabe
1 tablespoon virgin olive oil
1 medium onion, sliced
2 garlic cloves, sliced
  salt and black pepper to taste

Remove the flowers and leaves from the stems. Wash the broccoli rabe by submerging in cold water, lifting out of the water, and letting the sand sink to the bottom of the bowl. Place in a colander and let drain.

Heat the olive oil in a large saucepan and sauté the onion and garlic until golden. Add the broccoli rabe, season with salt and pepper, and cook until tender over medium heat (approximately 8 to 10 minutes). Serve hot.

Olive Bread

Makes 3 loaves

2 tablespoons (2 envelopes) dry yeast
1¾ cups lukewarm water
1½ tablespoons virgin olive oil
2 tablespoons honey
1 teaspoon sugar
1 tablespoon salt
½ cup chopped pitted green olives
½ cup chopped pitted black olives
5 cups bread flour, sifted
½ cup bread flour for dusting

Dissolve the yeast in water and let stand 10 minutes. Add the next 6 ingredients to the yeast mixture and ferment 10 minutes.

Add the flour and mix 10 minutes at low speed with a dough hook. Dust the sides of the bowl with flour as you go, to make sure the dough doesn't stick.

Place in a greased stainless steel bowl and cover with plastic wrap. Let proof (rise) 1 hour or until double in size.

Place quarry tile or a baking stone in the oven and preheat to 400°.

Turn the dough out onto a floured work area and separate into 3 equal pieces. With a rolling pin, roll each piece into a rectangle 10 to 12 inches long, 5 inches wide and ½ inch thick. Place on a greased baking sheet. With a sharp knife, make slits 3 inches long across the width every 2 inches. Brush with olive oil. Let proof another 30 minutes. Bake directly on the quarry tile for 30 minutes or until golden. When finished, place on a baking rack so air can flow around the entire loaf, cooling quickly and evenly.

Pecan Pie

Makes one 10-inch pie

> 3 cups pastry flour
> ½ cup all-purpose shortening
> ¼ tablespoon salt
> ¼ cup cold water

Combine the flour and shortening, and rub together with your hands until you form walnut-sized nuggets. Dissolve the salt in water and add to the flour mixture. Mix only until the ingredients are combined; do not overmix or the crust will be mealy. Form the dough into a ball, wrap with plastic, and refrigerate 2 hours. Letting the dough rest like this helps make the crust more tender.

Roll the dough into a 12-inch circle. Fold in half, then lay over a 10-inch pie tin (folding the dough in half makes it easier to lift into the pie tin without breaking). With a knife, cut off excess dough around the edges. Place the pie tin in the refrigerator 20 minutes, again letting the dough rest.

> **FILLING**
> ½ cup butter
> 2 cups sugar
> ½ teaspoon salt
> 2 cups maple syrup
> 2 cups corn syrup
> 6 eggs

6   egg yolks
½   tablespoon vanilla
1½ cups chopped pecans

Preheat the oven to 350°.

Melt the butter with the sugar and salt over low heat until the sugar is dissolved. Add the maple and corn syrup to the butter mixture and bring to a boil. Remove from the heat. In a mixing bowl, beat the whole eggs, yolks, and vanilla. Into the eggs, whisk 1 cup of the liquid at a time, until the temperature of the eggs becomes the same as that of the liquid. Continually whip the mixture to make sure the eggs do not curdle. Let the filling cool.

Remove the pie tin from the refrigerator and sprinkle the pecans evenly on the bottom of the pie shell. Pour the filling into the pie shell. Bake 1 hour. Before removing the pie from the oven, shake to make sure it is firm. The filling should move only slightly when the pie is shaken.

HALLOWEEN MENU

Escarole and White Bean Soup

Pan-seared Tenderloin in a Pepper Sauce

Brussels Sprouts with Bacon and Onion

French Fries

Clover Rolls

Pumpkin Fritters

WE USUALLY THINK OF HALLOWEEN as the quintessential children's holiday, but it is becoming more and more popular with adults as well. It's the one night of the year that it's acceptable for you to let the rest of the world see part of yourself that you keep hidden inside a corner. You want to play the werewolf, the athlete, the movie star, or the politician? This is the night to do it.

As kids, we usually went out door-to-door and collected bags of candy—much more than was good for us. Think of this Halloween menu as being a little bit like all that candy. We know there is a lot of fat in these dishes; in fact, we had to battle it out over whether to include it or not. But it's Halloween. Let's be like kids again for a day.

Escarole and White Bean Soup

6 servings

This is a very hearty soup that can stand on its own with fresh-baked bread. It is a perfect example of an Italian country meal. My grandmother didn't know this, but she was giving me everything I needed in one bowl!

- 3 cups white beans (soaked overnight)
- 1 tablespoon salt
- 2 bay leaves
- 2 whole cloves
- 1 tablespoon virgin olive oil
- 2 medium onions, thinly sliced
- 4 garlic cloves, thinly sliced
- 10 tomatoes, peeled and seeded
- 2 heads escarole, cleaned and shredded
- 1 tablespoon oregano
- 2 quarts chicken stock
- salt and black pepper to taste
- flavored oils for garnish (roasted garlic oil and chili oil work especially well)

Drain the beans and place in a large stockpot. Cover with 1 gallon water, and add the salt, bay leaves, and whole cloves. Boil about 45 minutes. Do not overcook the beans. They will finish cooking later, in the soup.

Heat the olive oil and sauté the onions and garlic until golden. Add the tomatoes, escarole, and oregano, and simmer 15 minutes. Add the beans and chicken stock and continue simmering another 30 minutes, or until the beans are completely tender. Salt and pepper to taste. Drizzle your favorite flavored oil over the soup. The tastes blend together, forming a marriage of different flavors.

Pan-seared Tenderloin in a Pepper Sauce

4 servings

4   6-ounce tenderloin steaks
1   tablespoon black peppercorns, cracked
1   tablespoon green peppercorns, cracked
1   tablespoon virgin olive oil
1   tablespoon shallots, chopped
1   tablespoon cider vinegar
1   tablespoon soy sauce
2   cups beef stock
1   cup heavy cream

Rub the steaks with the black and green peppercorns. In a heavy skillet, heat the olive oil over high heat. When the pan is hot, sear the steak for 2 minutes on each side, sealing in the juices. Remove the steak from the skillet and set aside.

Turn the heat down to medium, add the shallots, and cook until they begin to caramelize. Deglaze with the cider vinegar and soy sauce. Reduce until the pan is nearly dry; then add the beef stock. Reduce by half again and add the cream. Reduce again by half and return the steak to the skillet, being sure to add the juices that are left on the plate. Finish cooking about 4 minutes until medium rare. If you like your meat medium rare, when done it should feel soft with a spring to the touch, but not spongy. The more well done the steak is, the firmer it will feel to the touch. Serve the tenderloin covered with the sauce.

Brussels Sprouts with Bacon and Onion

4 servings

4   cups brussels sprouts
1   cup uncooked diced bacon (about 4 slices)
1   onion, diced
    salt and black pepper to taste

Cook the brussels sprouts in a large pot of boiling salted water for 6 to 8 minutes. Drain and set aside.

Cook the bacon at a low temperature, rendering until golden. Remove the bacon from the fat and discard the fat. In the same pan, sauté the onion until golden. Add the bacon and brussels sprouts, and season with salt and pepper to taste. Continue cooking about 4 to 6 minutes, or until thoroughly heated, and serve.

French Fries

4 servings

6   Yukon Gold potatoes
2   pounds shortening
    salt to taste

Wash, peel, and cut the potatoes into ½ inch strips. Place the potatoes in water until you are ready to cook so they do not turn brown. Heat the shortening in a large skillet to 350° (using a candy thermometer). When you are ready to fry, drain the potatoes and pat dry so that the oil doesn't spatter. Place the potatoes as close to the surface of the hot shortening as possible to minimize the risk of splashing. Blanch the potatoes in the shortening until they begin to turn golden. Remove from the shortening and cool. When ready to serve, lower into the hot shortening at about 400° and fry 4 minutes to finish cooking. The partial frying followed by the second frying is what makes french fries crisp. When deep frying, I use shortening. Some chefs prefer peanut oil or lard. I do very little deep frying, so my experience is limited. When the potatoes are done, remove them from the hot shortening, drain, and place on absorbent paper. Pat dry, sprinkle with a little salt, and serve immediately.

One of my favorite sauces for french fries is:

1   cup mayonnaise
½   cup ketchup
4   tablespoons cider vinegar

Whisk together to make a sweet-and-sour dipping sauce.

Clover Rolls

Makes 12 rolls

3	tablespoons (3 envelopes) dry yeast
1¾	cups lukewarm water
1	tablespoon salt
½	cup sugar
½	cup powdered buttermilk
½	cup butter, melted
5	cups bread flour, sifted
½	cup bread flour for dusting
	egg wash: 2 eggs lightly beaten with 2 tablespoons water
1	tablespoon dried thyme
1	tablespoon kosher salt
1	teaspoon black pepper

Dissolve the yeast in water and let stand 10 minutes. Add the salt, sugar, buttermilk, and butter to the yeast mixture and ferment another 10 minutes.

Add the flour to the liquid and mix with a dough hook 10 minutes at low speed, dusting with bread flour to make sure the dough does not stick to the sides of the bowl.

Place in a greased stainless steel bowl, cover with plastic wrap, and let proof (rise) 1 hour or until double in size. Turn the dough out onto a floured work area and divide into 36 equal pieces. With the palms of your hand, roll each piece into a ball. Grease a 12-cup muffin tin. Place 3 balls in each muffin cup. Proof (let rise) for 1 hour or until double in size.

Preheat the oven to 400° while the rolls are proofing.

Bake 15 minutes. Remove the rolls, lower the oven temperature to 350°, brush the rolls quickly with egg wash, and sprinkle with thyme, salt, and pepper. Bake another 15 minutes. Remove from the oven and turn onto a baking rack to cool.

Pumpkin Fritters

Makes 24 fritters

- 1 cup granulated sugar
- 1 cup brown sugar, packed
- 6 cups all-purpose flour
- 2 tablespoons baking powder
- 1 teaspoon salt
- 2 teaspoons ground cinnamon
- 1 teaspoon ground cardamom
- ½ teaspoon mace
- 1 cup butter, melted
- 4 eggs
- 2 cups pumpkin puree
- 1 cup buttermilk
- 2 pounds shortening (for frying)
- 2 cups powdered sugar

In a large mixing bowl, combine the granulated sugar, brown sugar, flour, baking powder, salt, cinnamon, cardamom, and mace. In a separate bowl, combine the melted butter, eggs, pumpkin, and buttermilk. Add the wet ingredients to the dry, and mix well. Let the dough rest 20 minutes.

In the meantime, heat the shortening in a large heavy skillet (I prefer to use cast iron) until it reaches 360° on a candy thermometer (or until a drop of water placed in the hot shortening dances across the top).

With a large tablespoon, drop spoonfuls of dough into the hot frying liquid a few at a time, making sure the fritter is cooked on all sides. Stir occasionally to avoid pale spots. Remove the fritter from the frying liquid and place on absorbent paper to drain.

Dust heavily with powdered sugar and serve warm. I like to place a few fritters in a paper bag, add powdered sugar, and shake, making sure the sugar clings to all sides.

THANKSGIVING DINNER

Roast Turkey with Honey Glaze

Corn Bread and Sausage Dressing

Cranberry-Orange Relish

Baked Sweet Potatoes

Broccoli and Spinach Casserole

Pumpkin Cheesecake

THANKSGIVING IS A HOLIDAY EVERYONE CAN ENJOY. Most families serve turkey, but what makes each dinner distinctive is the accompanying dishes. We can tell our different ethnic and economic backgrounds from the glazes we use and the desserts we serve. Thanksgiving represents the wholeness of the family. Although there have been difficulties, we put them past us and share the gifts a Higher Power has brought us in a gathering of mutual gratitude. When using, I could never go past the resentments and feel part of my family. Today, the gratitude I feel for the chance to see myself as an equal in my family, and to share the happiness and sadness of my family, is a gift I could not repay.

I remember going to family Thanksgiving dinners and my mother and aunts would say, "Poor Gino." My cousins would say I was a bum lacking willpower. Today I am considered an equal; my relatives ask me what I think about a situation or how I would handle it.

One of the ways I like to show my gratitude is by hosting the Thanksgiving dinner. Providing an atmosphere of mutual respect, we can share with one another openly, feeding our souls, giving us the two basic ingredients of life: human contact and food.

Roast Turkey with Honey Glaze

8 servings

1   16-pound turkey, neck bone and giblets set aside
1   onion, quartered
2   celery stalks, coarsely chopped
2   carrots, coarsely chopped
1   bay leaf
1   tablespoon dried thyme
2   quarts chicken stock
2   cups all-purpose flour

In the bottom of a roasting pan, put the neck bone and giblets, onion, celery, carrots, bay leaf, thyme, and 1 quart chicken stock.

Preheat the oven to 350°. Put the turkey on a rack in the roasting pan and roast. Meanwhile prepare the glaze (see page 174). After 1 hour, brush the turkey with the honey glaze. Repeat every 20 minutes until the turkey is done (2 to 3 hours). The turkey should register 180° internally on a meat thermometer when it is fully cooked, and the breast meat will pull away from the bone. The turkey drippings plus the vegetables and stock will be used later to make a delicious sauce.

When the bird is done, set it aside to cool and pour the drippings, including the neck bone and giblets, into a saucepan. Bring to a boil and skim off excess fat to use for roux. Add the remaining quart of chicken stock, and simmer 1 hour.

While the sauce is simmering, make the roux: Place the turkey fat in a sauté pan over medium heat and gradually add 2 cups all-purpose flour, stirring continuously. Cook until the aroma is nutty and the roux becomes a blond color. Set the roux aside to cool. When cool, whisk into the simmering sauce with a wire whisk,

COOKING TIP: *When using a roux, the roux has to be cool and the stock has to be hot, or the roux hot and the stock cool. If they are both the same temperature, you will have lumps. In the kitchen we call this a liaison, bringing two things together to form one. One has to compromise with the other to make a delicious sauce!*

making sure there are no lumps. Continue simmering 1 hour, tasting occasionally. If there is a raw flour taste, continue cooking until the taste has disappeared. Adjust seasoning at the end with salt and pepper. Strain through a fine-mesh sieve.

HONEY GLAZE

- 1 tablespoon virgin olive oil
- 1 onion, chopped
- ½ cup sugar
- 1 cup honey
- 1 cup orange juice, preferably fresh squeezed
- 12 oranges, peeled and sectioned
- 1 tablespoon chili oil (see page 84)

Heat the olive oil in a saucepan and sauté the onion until translucent. Add the sugar, stirring over medium heat. When it becomes golden, add the honey and orange juice, stirring and cooking until a syrup forms. Add the orange sections and cook until the syrup coats the back of the spoon. Finish with the chili oil. Brush onto the turkey every 20 minutes during the last hour of cooking.

GARLIC-ROSEMARY GLAZE VARIATION

This glaze gives the turkey a more Italian touch, making it more personal for me.

- 2 tablespoons virgin olive oil
- 4 garlic cloves, thinly sliced
- 1 cup sugar
- 1 cup chicken stock
- 1 tablespoon dried rosemary

In the olive oil, sauté the garlic until translucent. Add the sugar. Stir continuously, cooking over medium heat. When the mixture becomes golden, add the stock. Stir vigorously and continue cooking until the mixture coats the back of the spoon. Finish with the rosemary and brush the turkey as above.

Corn Bread and Sausage Dressing

8 servings

1 loaf white bread
1 loaf corn bread
1 tablespoon virgin olive oil
1 onion, chopped
2 garlic cloves, chopped
2 stalks celery, chopped
1 leek, chopped
1 tablespoon dried sage
1 teaspoon thyme
1 tablespoon black pepper
2 tablespoons salt
1 pound sweet Italian sausage without casing
2 cups milk
4 eggs
2 cups chicken stock

Preheat the oven to 350°.

Cut the white bread into ½-inch cubes and place on a sheet pan. Toast in the oven until golden (about 4 minutes). Crumble the corn bread onto a baking sheet and dry in the oven until the crumbs are toasty (2 to 5 minutes; you'll have to keep an eye on them so they don't burn). Set aside.

Heat the olive oil and sauté the onion until translucent. Add the garlic and continue cooking 3 to 4 minutes. Add the celery, leek, sage, thyme, pepper, and salt. Cook 4 to 6 minutes; then transfer to a large mixing bowl.

In the same pan used to cook the onion and garlic, cook the sausage at medium heat, rendering the fat. Stir occasionally. When done, place in a colander to drain excess fat. Add the sausage, toasted white bread, and crumbled corn bread to the vegetables in the mixing bowl and combine thoroughly.

In a small bowl, whisk together the milk, eggs, and stock. Add to the stuffing mixture and mix well. Place in a greased roasting pan and bake 1 hour.

Some people like to stuff the turkey. If you do, you must let the stuffing cool before stuffing the bird (otherwise the warm stuffing encourages bacteria growth before the heat of the oven reaches the inner bird). I don't stuff my turkeys because I want to avoid the risk of food-borne illness. When cooking the bird stuffed, the stuffing temperature is between 40° and 140° (which is referred to as the danger zone) for too long a period, which allows bacteria growth to double and triple every 30 seconds. Some say this bacteria growth gives the stuffing its unique flavor, but I like to play it safe!

Cranberry-Orange Relish

6 servings

2	pounds fresh cranberries
7	oranges
1	bay leaf
2	cinnamon sticks
2	whole cloves
4	cups sugar
2	quarts water
2	tablespoons cornstarch
2	tablespoons cold water

Peel the oranges using a paring knife: cut away the peel and the white membrane. Reserve the peel from one orange. Cut the oranges into wedges, cutting the flesh away from the core to leave beautiful, bright orange sections free of membrane. Squeeze the remaining orange cores and membranes to extract the juice, and reserve the orange sections and juice.

Put the cranberries, orange peel, bay leaf, cinnamon sticks, cloves, sugar, and 2 quarts of water into a stockpot. Bring to a boil; then turn the temperature down and simmer until the cranberries are soft. Drain the cranberries, saving the liquid in a saucepan. Purée half the cranberries, leaving the rest whole. Set aside. Simmer the liquid until it reduces to a syrup (about 1 hour). Dissolve the cornstarch in the 2 tablespoons cold water and add it to the liquid to thicken. Remove the bay leaf, cinnamon sticks, cloves, and orange peel, and add the cranberries, orange sections, and juice to the syrup. Stir and set aside to cool. Serve at room temperature.

Baked Sweet Potatoes

8 servings

8   sweet potatoes (about 5 pounds), peeled and diced
1   cup butter, melted
½   cup brown sugar
½   cup maple syrup
1   tablespoon salt
1   teaspoon black pepper
1   teaspoon cardamom
½   teaspoon nutmeg

Preheat the oven to 350°, and bring a large pot of water to boil.

Cook the sweet potatoes in the boiling water until tender, about 8 minutes. Drain, then puree the sweet potatoes in a food processor, or mash by hand the old-fashioned way. Add the butter, brown sugar, maple syrup, salt, pepper, cardamom, and nutmeg, and mix well. Place in an oiled baking dish, bake for 30 minutes, and serve.

Broccoli and Spinach Casserole

8 servings

4   bunches of spinach, washed
4   heads fresh broccoli, washed and trimmed
1   tablespoon virgin olive oil
1   onion, diced
2   garlic cloves, finely chopped
4   eggs
2   cups milk
2   cups fresh white breadcrumbs (see page 27)
1   tablespoon salt
1   teaspoon black pepper
1   teaspoon nutmeg
1   cup feta cheese, crumbled

Preheat the oven to 350°.

Steam the spinach for 2 minutes, squeeze out the excess water, and chop. Steam the broccoli for 3 minutes, drain, and coarsely chop.

Heat the olive oil and sauté the onion and garlic until translucent; then transfer to a large mixing bowl. Add the eggs, milk, breadcrumbs, salt, pepper, and nutmeg. Mix well, place in an oiled baking dish, sprinkle with feta cheese, and bake 45 minutes. Let the casserole stand for 20 minutes; then serve.

Pumpkin Cheesecake

Makes two 10-inch cakes

I like to use cheese pumpkin because this variety is sweeter, less stringy, and higher in starch, making it excellent for baking. This crustless cheesecake makes a delightful variation on the traditional pumpkin pie.

1	cheese pumpkin (about 5 pounds)
	virgin olive oil
	salt
4	cups sugar
2	cups butter
6	cups cream cheese
1	cup sour cream
4	eggs
4	egg yolks
2	cups all-purpose flour
1	teaspoon vanilla
¼	teaspoon mace
¼	teaspoon nutmeg
½	teaspoon allspice

Cut the pumpkin into quarters, scoop out the seeds, rub with olive oil, and sprinkle with salt. Roast at 400° for 45 minutes or until tender. Let cool and scoop out the pulp. Purée the pulp and set aside.

Lower the oven temperature to 350°.

In the work bowl of a heavy-duty mixer, cream together the sugar and butter, using the paddle attachment. When smooth, add the cream cheese and continue mixing until smooth. Add the sour cream, eggs, and egg yolks slowly, making sure all the liquid is incorporated. Add the flour and pumpkin purée, and mix until blended. Add the vanilla, mace, nutmeg, and allspice, and blend.

Pour the batter into two 10-inch springform pans, filling the pans only two-thirds full. Place the 2 cake pans in a large roasting pan, and pour water into the roasting pan until the water level comes halfway up the cake pans. Bake 1 hour; then turn off the oven and let the cheesecakes rest in the oven for another hour. This is so the cake can set and become firm enough to slice. Remove from the oven, let cool, remove springform pan, and refrigerate.

When thoroughly cooled, slice and serve. Before making each incision, dip the knife into hot water.

THOUGHTS ON RECOVERY

So much of my addiction involved my separation from family, friends, and surroundings. By enjoying a diet based on the seasons and using local products, I am able to become closer to the ones I love and to my surroundings. As a child I learned tools to keep me in touch with the creative force and tools to maintain good health. For example, we used to roast pumpkin seeds after we carved the pumpkins. We didn't know that they were an excellent source of protein and iron and low in fat. We just thought they tasted good.

Eating foods produced in our area helps keep our bodies in tune with the earth. Technology ought to enhance our life, not change it. We were meant to eat local products to receive full nutritional value from what we are eating. So many things brought to the market from faraway places change the chemistry of the foods through techniques of shipping, such as gassing tomatoes so they will have a bright-red color when we receive them and picking fruits before they are ripe so they do not bruise in shipping. Technology changes but our bodies stay the same, created by love in a perfect way. Through the centuries, our needs have remained the same: love, food, and community.

One of the ways I feel part of my community is by sharing the food I create with the people I love. I take what God gives me and I try to enhance it, keeping it simple, never trying to overshadow the natural goodness of fresh, God-given ingredients.

The staff at Hazelden meet together over pizza.

Winter

There are two keys to preparing a good soup:
fresh ingredients and time.

Mushroom-Barley Soup

Carrot-Ginger Soup

*White Chocolate Mousse
in Tulip Cups*

CHRISTMAS EVE BUFFET

Pan-fried Fillet of Sole with Warm Red Lentil Salad   *Sautéed Escarole*
Sautéed Shrimp in Spicy Tomato Sauce with Fettuccine
Fried Calamari with Spicy Yogurt Sauce   *Roasted Garlic Corn Muffins*
Macaroons   *Sugar Cookies Filled with Raisins and Almonds*

Thanksgiving is over and you can feel the excitement
of the holiday season lighting upon us. Christmas shopping, family gatherings, and a host of responsibilities can be overwhelming. What I like to do is keep it simple, trying to remember what we are celebrating, not getting lost in the hype. I try to remember what is most important, staying sober and helping other people.

Growing up in an Italian home, Christmas Eve was always a special event. We never got much sleep. We would start the evening with a seafood buffet and then go to midnight mass. When we returned, we began to prepare for Christmas dinner, tend to last-minute gift wrapping, and play cards until early morning.

There seemed to be a spirit that came into the house. I could never really pinpoint when it arrived, but I would feel its presence there. It would start in my grandmother's kitchen and spread throughout the house, like the aromas of the foods she was preparing. Her food embodied her emotions, the way she shared her warmth and love with her family.

I lost that sense of family security when I started using, but the program has given it back to me. In early recovery, I always felt so uncomfortable during the holidays, not knowing how to behave, never knowing what I liked, always thinking I should be doing something other than what I was doing.

Now I realize what brings me comfort: being in my home and surrounding myself with family and friends, celebrating the best gift of all—one another's company. I can look back on the year and see how my life has grown and changed. Like a tree, life continually grows and changes, and watching the changes gives me a feeling of wonderment and excitement about what could be.

The Winter Market

The party is over; it's time to go inside. During the winter, I spend more time in the kitchen, experimenting with new ideas and preparing old favorites. It is a time of reflection and hope. The selection is somewhat limited, but winter vegetables with their unique flavors and versatility make up the difference. They might be imperfect, but together they complement each other in countless ways.

Winter seems forever, but the days eventually become longer, the temperature begins to rise, and we feel the internal hope of spring.

Some of the produce waiting at the market for us are winter greens such as kale, collard greens, and broccoli rabe, and root vegetables such as Belgian endive, celery root, parsnips, and a variety of potatoes.

Most winter produce is best stored at 55 degrees, covered and in a dark place. You can store winter vegetables for longer periods of time than spring, summer, and autumn vegetables. The reason for storing winter vegetables covered and in a dark place is that oxygen and ultraviolet light deplete the nutrients and minerals.

BELGIAN ENDIVE A white-leafed, bitter vegetable with a distinctive flavor, belgian endive is delicious braised. Endive is best stored in a plastic bag in the refrigerator if you will not be using it for several days. If the outer layers turn brown, peel them off and cut the round white core. When washing endive, do not soak it because the nutrients will leak into the water causing the endive to become bitter.

CELERY ROOT Celery root should be stored in the bottom of the refrigerator at 55 degrees. When wrapped in plastic, it can be stored for a week to 10 days. It has a brown, knobby, coarse exterior, but beneath this is a very tender, delicious heart. Celery root and potato are a perfect combination in both soups and purées. When picking out celery root, look for a distinctive aroma, indicating freshness.

FENNEL Fennel brings a light touch to winter, both as an herb and as a vegetable. Growing up we would have it fresh and eat it raw as if it were a summer vegetable. In my family we used fennel any way we could—braised, sautéed, or accompanying seafood, veal, or poultry. When storing, cut away the leaves and stalk, wrap in plastic, and it will keep for a week, easily.

ONIONS Onions are stored in the bottom of the refrigerator or in a vegetable box. They will store for long periods (up to two weeks). When buying onions, make sure the skin is brittle and dry. They should be firm and compact.

PARSNIPS Parsnips are very high in sugar content and can be used in various ways, from sliced and baked for appetizers to baked in breads and cakes. When shopping for parsnips, pick out ones that are ivory in color and firm and have no brown spots. If you're looking for a high-calorie snack, parsnips, thinly sliced and deep-fried, make a wonderful chip!

POTATOES *White potatoes* are all-purpose potatoes, similar to red potatoes. Their taste and texture make them excellent for boiling and sautéing.

Red potatoes are thin-skinned potatoes; their colors range from pink to red. They are also labeled "new" potatoes. Their firm, waxy texture makes them excellent for boiling and roasting and for whenever the potato needs to keep its shape—for example, in a potato salad.

Russet potatoes are oblong, brown, and thin-skinned. The texture of their meat is fluffy, making them an excellent baking potato.

Yukon Gold potatoes are great for making mashed potatoes or for thickening soups because they are more starchy, therefore sweeter.

SWEET POTATOES Another versatile root vegetable, sweet potatoes can be used in pies, soups, purées, and breads.

At home I have a small refrigerator (or vegetable box) that I keep between 50 and 55 degrees to store my root vegetables. Do not store potatoes or other vegetables in any colder temperature because they start to break down and turn their starch into sugar. If you don't have the luxury of having a vegetable box, keep your winter vegetables covered and stored in the bottom of your refrigerator.

One of the things I like to do when entertaining is make my own bowl of chips, using an assortment of root vegetables. I use potatoes, sweet potatoes, yucca, parsnips, and turnips. I peel them and slice them as thinly as possible. I use a slicing tool called a mandolin. I deep-fry the slices at 350 degrees until they start to turn color. With a slotted spoon, I remove them and put them on absorbent paper. Placed in a decorative bowl in the center of the table, they make a very eye-catching snack with all their varied colors.

No other seasonal produce can be used in as many different ways as the winter market produce.

HEARTY STOCKS AND SOUPS

Stocks
Vegetable Stock
Chicken Stock
Brown Beef Stock
Fish Stock

Soups
Cabbage and Potato Soup
Mushroom-Barley Soup
Purée of Cauliflower and Potato Soup
Lentil and Escarole Soup
Shrimp Bisque
Black Bean Soup
Carrot-Ginger Soup

AT THE CULINARY INSTITUTE, one of the first principles of cooking I learned was *mise en place*, which is French for "everything in its place." You can be the most creative chef in the world, but if you're not organized, you will not be able to execute your ideas. It's the same principle behind the slogan First things first. If you don't begin with a solid foundation, everything will collapse.

The same is true with soup: If you don't start with a good stock, your soup will never live up to its potential. It will always be missing something. No matter how you try to season it, it will always lack its proper foundation.

There are two keys to preparing a good stock: fresh ingredients and time. Letting the stock simmer for a long period extracts the flavors and proteins from the bones, giving the stock its unique flavor, body, and velvety smooth texture.

There are a few other simple guidelines to follow when making homemade stock. Always start your stock with cold water. This will help ensure that you end up with a clear stock. Warm water can make the blood from the bones bleed into your stock. You want to cook the stock gently. Never let the stock boil; just let it come to a simmer. From time to time add a cup of cold water to reduce the temperature of the stock. This allows you to skim the impurities that rise to the top, creating a beautifully clear stock. To skim, run a ladle over the stock, holding the edge of the ladle a fraction of an inch below the surface so the fat and other impurities flow into the ladle.

One of the nice things about stock is that you get to use the bones you might otherwise throw away. Nothing is wasted. You can prepare stock, chill it, and then freeze it in small portions to use later, adding richness to whatever you are preparing.

If you don't have time to prepare your own stocks, there are several alternatives, although they just aren't quite as good. You can use chicken or beef bouillon cubes, or liquid stock base, following the package instructions for preparation. Or you can use canned stocks. All of these options tend to be a little salty. Gourmet stores often have frozen stocks available for purchase. These can be more expensive, but the quality is usually high.

Vegetable Stock

Yield: 1 gallon

A vegetable stock can be rich with vitamins when you use a variety of aromatic vegetables in the preparation. Vegetable stocks take less time to prepare than meat stocks; you should not cook vegetable stock too long or it will become bitter. You can replace chicken stock with vegetable stock any time you want a vegetarian meal. It is also naturally lower in fat than meat stock.

- 2 tablespoons virgin olive oil
- 2 cups onions, sliced
- 2 cups washed chopped leeks (green and white parts)
- 1 cup chopped celery
- 2 cups chopped carrots
- 1 cup chopped turnips
- 2 cups chopped fresh tomatoes
- 4 garlic cloves, sliced
- 5 quarts cold water
- 1 bay leaf
- 2 sprigs fresh thyme
- 2 whole cloves
- 1 tablespoon salt

In a large stockpot, heat the olive oil and add the onions, leeks, celery, carrots, turnips, tomatoes, and garlic. Sweat 10 to 12 minutes over medium heat to extract the natural flavors. Add the cold water, bay leaf, thyme, cloves, and salt. Simmer 40 minutes. Strain the stock and cool immediately.

Chicken Stock

Yield: 1 gallon

10	pounds chicken bones (see note)
6	quarts cold water
1	cup diced onions
1	cup diced carrots
1	cup diced celery
1	cup diced leeks (white part only)
1	bay leaf
2	sprigs fresh thyme
2	whole cloves
1	tablespoon salt

Combine the chicken bones and water in a large stockpot. Slowly bring to a simmer, skimming off the impurities. Simmer 3 hours.

Add the onions, carrots, celery, leeks, bay leaf, thyme, cloves, and salt. Simmer another hour, continuing to skim occasionally to ensure a clear stock. Add a cup of cold water from time to time to help bring the impurities to the top (do this 2 or 3 times).

VARIATION

For brown chicken stock, put the chicken bones in a large roasting pan. Brush with 2 cups of tomato paste, place in the oven, and roast at 400° until the bones are caramelized, about 1 hour. Then put the chicken bones in 6 quarts of cold water and proceed as above.

NOTE: You can purchase chicken bones from your butcher, or you can save the backs and necks from chickens you have boned at home. You can also use the carcass of a whole chicken you have roasted, but the flavor will be different.

Brown Beef Stock

Yield: 1 gallon

10   pounds veal bones
 1   calf's foot, split
 5   pounds ox tail, cut into 2-inch pieces
 2   cups tomato paste
 2   gallons cold water
 2   cups chopped onions
 2   cups chopped carrots
 1   cup chopped celery
 1   cup chopped leeks (white and green parts)
 1   bay leaf
 2   sprigs fresh thyme
 2   whole cloves
 1   tablespoon salt

Preheat the oven to 400°.

Set the bones in a large roasting pan and brush with the tomato paste. Roast in the oven for 2 hours.

Combine the bones with water in a 4-gallon stockpot. Bring to a simmer slowly, skimming the impurities as they rise. Simmer for 10 hours (see note). Add an additional cup of cold water 2 or 3 times. This will help impurities rise to the top so you can skim them away.

Add the onions, carrots, celery, leeks, bay leaf, thyme, cloves, and salt. Simmer for another hour, strain, and chill.

NOTE: If you do not have the luxury of staying home all day to watch this liquid turn into a glorious stock, you can cook it in segments. Each time you return it to the stove, however, you have to bring it to a boil and then let it simmer. You can also make the stock in a crockpot, or leave it to cook overnight, simmering at a low temperature.

Fish Stock

Yield: 1 gallon

- 6 pounds flat fish bones (see note)
- 5 quarts cold water
- 1 cup diced onions
- 1 cup diced celery
- 1 cup diced leeks (white part only)
- 1 bay leaf
- 2 sprigs thyme
- 2 whole cloves
- 1 tablespoon salt

Combine the bones and water in a large stockpot and simmer 30 minutes.

Add the onions, celery, leeks, bay leaf, thyme, cloves, and salt. Simmer another 30 minutes, skimming from time to time. Strain and chill.

NOTE: Use only flat bones such as those from sole or flounder because anything else has too strong a flavor. You can usually get fish bones from a fish market or the seafood counter of better grocery stores.

Cabbage and Potato Soup

6 servings

- 2 tablespoons virgin olive oil
- 2 onions, thinly sliced
- 4 garlic cloves, thinly sliced
- 1 head green cabbage (about 2 pounds)
- 2 tablespoons sugar
- 2 tablespoons salt
- 10 medium potatoes, peeled and diced (cook separately until slightly underdone)
- 1 cup cider vinegar

        2 quarts chicken stock (or vegetable stock)
        1 bay leaf
        1 cup chopped fresh dill (or 2 tablespoons dried dill)
        2 teaspoons black pepper

Heat the olive oil in a large stockpot and sauté the onions over medium heat until they become golden and begin to caramelize. Add the garlic and continue cooking about 4 minutes.

Cut the cabbage in half, remove the core, and cut the cabbage into 2-inch pieces. Add the cabbage to the stockpot.

When the cabbage begins to wilt, add the sugar and salt and continue cooking, stirring occasionally, letting the cabbage and sugar caramelize.

When the cabbage is golden, deglaze with the vinegar, scraping the bottom of the pot, making sure to soften up the rich caramel on the bottom. Add the stock, bay leaf, dill, and pepper. Simmer 40 minutes. After the first 20 minutes, cook the potatoes in a separate pot of boiling water until they are slightly underdone (about 10 minutes). Drain the starchy water and add the potatoes to the simmering soup for the remaining 10 minutes.

Serve with a garnish of fresh chopped dill.

Mushroom-Barley Soup

6 servings

The combination of the caramelized vegetables and the tomato paste gives a distinct flavor. Later, combining them with the stock creates a rich and velvety texture that can only be achieved by this technique.

        1 cup raw barley
        2 tablespoons virgin olive oil
        4 diced carrots
        2 diced celery stalks
        2 leeks (white part only), diced

2 onions, diced
2 garlic cloves, diced
1 cup tomato paste
1 cup cider vinegar
1 quart chicken stock and 1 quart brown beef stock
   (or 2 quarts vegetable stock)
1 bay leaf
2 sprigs fresh thyme (or 2 teaspoons dried thyme)
   salt and black pepper
4 cups mushrooms (about a pound), sliced
2 tablespoons cornstarch
   juice of 1 lemon

Combine the barley with 4 cups salted water and simmer, covered, for 45 minutes, or until the barley is cooked but still slightly firm.

While the barley is cooking, heat 1 tablespoon olive oil in a large sauté pan and sauté the carrots and celery over medium heat until they begin to caramelize. Add the leeks, onions, and garlic. Continue cooking 6 to 12 minutes, letting all the vegetables begin to turn golden and caramelize.

Add the tomato paste, and continue to cook over medium heat, stirring occasionally, so that the paste loses its acidity and becomes sweeter.

Deglaze with the vinegar in 3 stages before adding the stocks. Add ⅓ cup of the vinegar at a time, making sure all the liquid has evaporated before adding the next ⅓ cup. Add the chicken and beef stocks, bay leaf, thyme, salt and pepper, and simmer 1 hour.

Meanwhile, sauté the mushrooms in 1 tablespoon olive oil until the mushrooms become soft. Sprinkle with salt and pepper to taste.

Add the mushrooms and barley to the soup and simmer another 10 minutes.

Mix the cornstarch with 2 tablespoons cold water, making sure there are no lumps, and then slowly add this mixture to the soup. Make sure the soup comes to a boil before you add the cornstarch. This helps bind the soup to the vegetables so they do not sink to the bottom but remain suspended evenly throughout the liquid. Season with the lemon juice and serve.

Purée of Cauliflower and Potato Soup

6 servings

1	tablespoon virgin olive oil
2	onions, thinly sliced
2	leeks (white part only), diced
4	garlic cloves, sliced
3	heads cauliflower, cleaned and cut into florets
6	potatoes, peeled and diced (see note)
2	celery roots, peeled and diced
2	quarts vegetable stock
1	tablespoon salt
1	teaspoon pepper
½	teaspoon nutmeg
1	teaspoon dried thyme
1	cup heavy cream
1	sprig fresh parsley, chopped

Heat the olive oil in a large stockpot and sauté the onions, leeks, and garlic until translucent. Add the cauliflower, potatoes, and celery roots and continue cooking 6 to 8 minutes.

Add the stock and the salt, pepper, nutmeg, and thyme, and simmer about 30 minutes.

Strain the vegetables from the stock and purée them in a blender or food processor.

Return the puréed vegetables to the stock. Add the cream and continue simmering 10 minutes.

Serve garnished with a little chopped parsley.

NOTE: If you are not going to use the potatoes right away, hold them in cold water until ready. This prevents them from turning brown.

Lentil and Escarole Soup

6 servings

4	strips bacon, diced
1	small onion, diced
2	garlic cloves, diced
4	carrots, diced
1	leek (white part only), diced
2	tablespoons tomato paste
3	cups dried lentils
1	quart chicken stock
1	quart brown beef stock
1	teaspoon salt
½	teaspoon black pepper
1	bay leaf
2	teaspoons virgin olive oil
1	head escarole, washed and diced
	juice of 1 lemon
1	sprig thyme
1	tablespoon Italian (flat-leaf) parsley, chopped

In a large stockpot, cook the bacon over low heat until it begins to crisp. Add the onion and garlic and continue cooking until they become translucent. Add the carrots and leek and continue cooking 8 to 12 minutes over medium heat.

Add the tomato paste and simmer 6 minutes, stirring occasionally to make sure the tomato paste does not burn.

Add the lentils, stock, salt, pepper, and bay leaf, and simmer about 40 minutes, until the lentils are tender.

Heat 1 teaspoon of the olive oil in a large skillet and sauté the escarole. Add the escarole to the soup and continue simmering 6 to 8 minutes.

Finish with the lemon juice and the remaining 1 teaspoon olive oil. Garnish with the thyme and chopped parsley.

Shrimp Bisque

6 servings

When you cook with fresh shrimp, save all the shells in the freezer so you have them when you want to make shrimp bisque. This tasty soup is a great dish for using up shrimp shells that would otherwise go to waste.

- 2 tablespoons virgin olive oil
- 1 onion, diced
- 1 celery stalk, diced
- 2 leeks (white part only), diced
- 2 garlic cloves, diced
- 1 cup tomato paste
- 1 cup cider vinegar
- 1 pound shrimp shells
- 2 quarts fish stock
- 1 bay leaf
- 2 sprigs fresh tarragon (or 1 teaspoon dried tarragon)
- 1 tablespoon salt
- 1 teaspoon black pepper
- ½ teaspoon cayenne pepper
- 2 cups heavy cream
- 2 tablespoons cornstarch, dissolved in 2 tablespoons cold water
  juice of 1 lemon

Heat the olive oil in a large stockpot and sauté the onion, celery, leeks, and garlic over medium heat until they start to caramelize, about 6 to 8 minutes. Add the tomato paste and continue cooking over medium heat, caramelizing the tomato paste and stirring frequently to make sure it does not burn.

Deglaze with the vinegar in 3 stages. Add ⅓ cup of the vinegar at a time, making sure all the liquid has evaporated before adding the next ⅓ cup.

Add the shrimp shells and continue cooking 15 minutes. The shells will turn a reddish brown. Add the fish stock, bay leaf, tarragon, salt, pepper, and cayenne pepper and simmer 1 hour.

Strain the stock, making sure you squeeze all the juice out of the shells by pressing them with a ladle against a fine-mesh sieve. Return the stock to the stove, bring to a simmer, add the cream, and continue to simmer 10 to 12 minutes.

Bring the soup to a boil and gradually add the cornstarch mixture to thicken. Finish with the lemon juice.

VARIATION
To serve shrimp bisque as a one-dish meal, garnish with 12 ounces of shrimp that you've diced and sautéed with onion and garlic.

Black Bean Soup

6 servings

1 tablespoon virgin olive oil
2 cups black beans, soaked overnight in water
1 onion, diced
4 garlic cloves, chopped
2 celery stalks, diced
2 carrots, diced
2 leeks (white part only), diced
2 quarts chicken stock (or vegetable stock)
1 bay leaf
1 cup chopped cilantro
1 tablespoon salt
2 teaspoons black pepper
1 tablespoon chili oil (see page 84)
juice of 1 lemon
chopped red onions and sour cream (for garnish)

Heat the olive oil in a large stockpot and sauté the onion, garlic, celery, carrots, and leeks until the onion is translucent.

Drain and rinse the black beans, and then add to the vegetables. Add the stock, bay leaf, cilantro, salt, and pepper. Simmer 1½ hours, until the beans are soft.

Remove half the beans and purée them in a blender or food processor. Return the purée to the soup and stir. Season with the chili oil and lemon juice. You can garnish with chopped red onions and sour cream.

Carrot-Ginger Soup

6 servings

1	tablespoon virgin olive oil
1	onion, sliced
4	garlic cloves, sliced
2	leeks (white part only), sliced
10	carrots, peeled and diced
1	~~cup~~ *TBLSP* peeled and grated fresh ginger
2	quarts chicken or vegetable stock
1	bay leaf
2	sprigs fresh thyme(or 1 teaspoon dried thyme)
5	potatoes
	beet juice or fresh ginger for garnish
	salt and black pepper

CELERY

Heat the olive oil in a large stockpot and sauté the onion, garlic, and leeks until translucent. Add the carrots and ginger and continue cooking over medium heat 8 to 12 minutes. Add the stock, bay leaf, and thyme, and simmer 20 minutes.

While the soup is simmering, peel and dice the potatoes. Add them to the stock and continue cooking until the potatoes are soft.

Strain the vegetables from the stock and purée them in a blender or food processor. Return them to the soup and simmer another 10 minutes, stirring occasionally. Add salt and pepper to taste.

Top with a swirl of beet juice for a festive look, or garnish with fresh ginger cut into strips ⅛-inch wide and 1-inch long, stewed in honey and water until the ginger is soft. Simply sprinkle the ginger on top of the soup when ready to serve.

CHRISTMAS EVE BUFFET

Pan-fried Fillet of Sole with Warm Red Lentil Salad

Sautéed Shrimp in Spicy Tomato Sauce with Fettuccine

Fried Calamari with Spicy Yogurt Sauce

Sautéed Escarole

Roasted Garlic Corn Muffins

Macaroons

Sugar Cookies Filled with Raisins and Almonds

Gino checks out the selection at a fish market in Chinatown.

From my earliest memories, my family had a seafood buffet on Christmas Eve. It's an Italian tradition, perhaps because of the importance of the symbolism of the fish in the Catholic church. Certain odors and tastes can be very evocative, bringing you back to another time and place. The aroma of fresh fish and simmering spicy tomato sauce will always bring back memories of the Christmas Eves of my childhood.

My family still carries on that tradition. We gather together to prepare the sumptuous dishes, and afterward we go to midnight mass. We fast until the next day after receiving communion around noon. People have been doing this twelve-hour fast for centuries to get closer to their God.

Christmas is a time when we can reaffirm and strengthen our connections with each other. Every family has its own special rituals and traditions meant to signal the importance of those bonds and connections. In recovery we have an opportunity to select the best of those traditions and make them our own.

Pan-fried Fillet of Sole with Warm Red Lentil Salad

6 servings

PAN-FRIED FILLET OF SOLE

- 4 eggs, lightly beaten
- 1 tablespoon salt
- 1 teaspoon black pepper
- ½ teaspoon cayenne pepper
- 4 cups fresh breadcrumbs (see page 27)
- 6 4-ounce fillets of sole
- 1 tablespoon olive oil (or nonstick cooking spray)

Blend the eggs with the salt, pepper, and cayenne pepper in a shallow dish, and place the breadcrumbs in another dish. Dip each fillet of sole first into the egg, then into the breadcrumbs.

Heat the olive oil in a large frying pan and brown the fillets on both sides, about 3 minutes per side. If you want to reduce the fat calories, spray the pan with nonstick coating instead of using olive oil.

WARM RED LENTIL SALAD

2 cups dried red lentils
1 head garlic
4 tablespoons virgin olive oil
1 cup sliced red onion
1 tablespoon dried basil
1 cup sun-dried tomatoes, sliced
1 tablespoon balsamic vinegar
  juice of 1 lemon
1 tablespoon salt
1 teaspoon black pepper
  lemon slices

Bring a large pot of water to boil. Add the lentils and boil about 25 minutes, or until tender. Drain and let cool to room temperature.

Meanwhile, remove the outer papery skin on the head of garlic, place in a small baking dish, drizzle with the olive oil, and roast at 400° until soft. Remove the pulp and mash. Reserve the olive oil for later use.

In a large mixing bowl, combine the lentils with the roasted garlic, red onion, basil, sun-dried tomatoes, balsamic vinegar, lemon juice, salt, pepper, and the reserved olive oil. Place the salad on a large platter, arrange the fillet of sole on top, and garnish with sliced lemon.

Sautéed Shrimp in Spicy Tomato Sauce with Fettuccine

6 servings

I use Italian canned tomatoes not out of a sense of loyalty to my ancestry, but because the canning plants in Italy are much smaller than those in the United States, so they have to rely on quality, not on the amount they produce. They can the tomatoes at just the right time, having allowed the tomatoes to ripen on the vine. The temperature of canning is not too high, so the tomatoes retain their natural nutrients and body.

1½ pounds shrimp, peeled and deveined (see page 14)

MARINADE

4 tablespoons virgin olive oil

juice of 1 lemon

1 tablespoon salt

1 teaspoon black pepper

½ teaspoon cayenne pepper

½ teaspoon chili pepper flakes

SAUCE

1 tablespoon virgin olive oil

1 onion, thinly sliced

4 garlic cloves, thinly sliced

8 cups canned Italian whole tomatoes

1 bay leaf

1 tablespoon dried oregano

1 teaspoon salt

1 teaspoon black pepper

½ teaspoon cayenne pepper

1½ pounds fettuccine or tagliatelle

1 teaspoon chili oil (see page 90)

Prepare the marinade: In a large bowl, whisk together the olive oil, lemon juice, salt, black pepper, cayenne pepper, and chili pepper. Add the shrimp and marinate 2 hours.

Prepare the sauce: In an ovenproof saucepan, heat the olive oil and sauté the onion and garlic until translucent. Add the tomatoes and bay leaf, oregano, salt, black pepper, and cayenne pepper, and simmer 1 hour in the oven at 350°. The dry heat of the oven cuts the acidity of the tomatoes, resulting in a sweet and delicious sauce.

Bring 1 gallon of water to boil in a stockpot with 1 teaspoon salt and 1 teaspoon olive oil. Add the pasta and cook 6 to 8 minutes. Test the pasta for desired softness, drain, place in a mixing bowl, and add half the tomato sauce.

Assemble the dish: Remove the shrimp from the marinade and sauté over high heat 3 to 4 minutes. They should look slightly pink. Place the pasta on a serving platter, spread the shrimp over the top, and cover with the remaining tomato sauce. Drizzle with chili oil.

Fried Calamari with Spicy Yogurt Sauce

6 servings

FRIED CALAMARI

1 pound calamari

4 cups milk

4 cups cornmeal

2 cups fresh breadcrumbs (see page 27)

4 eggs

shortening for deep-frying

Cut the calamari into 2-inch strips and soak in the milk 2 hours.

Combine the cornmeal and breadcrumbs in a shallow bowl, and in a separate bowl, lightly beat the eggs. Remove the calamari from the milk, dip into the eggs, and then coat with the cornmeal mixture. Set aside.

Half-fill a heavy skillet with shortening and heat until it begins to smoke. Add the calamari, 4 to 6 pieces at a time. When golden, remove with a slotted spoon, place on absorbent paper, and continue the process until all the calamari are cooked.

SPICY YOGURT SAUCE

4 cups chili sauce

1 cup plain yogurt

4 tablespoons grated horseradish

juice of 1 lemon

juice of 1 orange

1 tablespoon salt

1 teaspoon black pepper

1 tablespoon hot sauce

Blend together the chili sauce, yogurt, horseradish, lemon and orange juice, salt, pepper, and hot sauce.

Place the sauce in a decorative bowl, set it in the middle of a large platter, and arrange the fried calamari around the bowl.

Sautéed Escarole

6 servings

- 3 heads escarole
- 4 tablespoons virgin olive oil
- 4 garlic cloves, thinly sliced
- 1 tablespoon salt
- 1 teaspoon black pepper

Remove the outer leaves of the escarole and cut into 2-inch pieces. Submerge in cold water and drain.

Heat 3 tablespoons of the olive oil in a sauté pan. Add the garlic and sauté until it begins to turn golden. Add the escarole and continue cooking 4 to 6 minutes and season with salt and pepper. When the escarole is tender, remove with a slotted spoon. Place in the center of a platter and drizzle with the remaining olive oil.

Roasted Garlic Corn Muffins

Makes 12 muffins

- 1 cup cornmeal
- 1 cup all-purpose flour
- 1½ teaspoons baking powder
- ½ teaspoon baking soda
- 1 teaspoon salt
- ⅓ cup sugar
- 1½ cups buttermilk
- ¼ cup maple syrup
- 1 egg, beaten
- ⅓ cup butter, melted
- 4 garlic cloves, roasted and puréed

Preheat the oven to 350°. Spray muffin cups with nonstick coating.

In a small bowl, sift together the cornmeal, flour, baking powder, baking soda, salt, and sugar. In another bowl, combine the buttermilk, maple syrup, egg, and butter.

Add the liquid to the dry ingredients and blend until just moistened. Add the puréed garlic and mix. Spoon the batter into the prepared muffin cups and bake 20 minutes or until the muffins are a deep, rich, golden color.

Macaroons

Makes 24 macaroons

>   2 cups sugar
>   3 cups almond paste (see note)
>   ½ cup corn syrup
>   1 teaspoon vanilla
>   1½ cups egg whites
>   ½ cup all-purpose flour
>   powdered sugar

Preheat the oven to 400°. Line 2 large baking sheets with parchment paper and grease with butter.

Cream together the sugar and almond paste. Add the corn syrup, vanilla, and egg whites. Add the flour and continue mixing. When the batter is smooth, fill a pastry bag fitted with a plain pastry tube. Pipe the paste in 2-inch diameter drops on the greased parchment paper.

Bake 10 minutes until golden. Let cool completely before removing from the pan with a spatula. Arrange the macaroons on a platter and sprinkle with powdered sugar.

NOTE: Almond paste is available in the baking section of grocery stores or the refrigerated section of co-ops.

CHOCOLATE MACAROONS

>   4 cups sugar
>   3 cups almond paste
>   1 cup cocoa powder
>   1 cup all-purpose flour
>   1 cup grated coconut
>   1½ cups egg whites (about 3 eggs)

Preheat the oven to 350°. Line 2 large baking sheets with parchment paper and grease with butter.

Blend the sugar and almond paste together to form a paste. Sift the cocoa powder and flour together and add to the paste. Add the coconut and egg whites and blend thoroughly.

Fill a pastry bag fitted with a plain pastry tube. Pipe paste in 2-inch diameter drops on the greased parchment paper. Bake about 15 minutes. Let cool completely before removing from the pan with a spatula.

Sugar Cookies Filled with Raisins and Almonds

Makes 28 cookies

4 cups all-purpose flour
1 cup sugar
1 teaspoon baking powder
2 cups butter (about 4 sticks)
½ cup milk
2 tablespoons honey
2 eggs

FILLING
1 cup chopped semisweet chocolate
3 cups raisins
1 cup toasted almonds
½ teaspoon cardamom
½ teaspoon cinnamon
1 cup apricot glaze (you may need to buy this in a specialty store)
egg wash: 1 egg lightly beaten with 1 teaspoon water
powdered sugar

Prepare the dough: In a stainless steel bowl, place the flour, sugar, baking powder, and butter. Rub together until you form walnut-sized pieces. In a separate mixing bowl, combine the milk, honey, and eggs. Add the wet ingredients to the dry and mix by hand until the dough forms a ball. Knead 3 or 4 minutes, but be careful not to overmix. Divide the dough into 14 pieces, wrap in plastic, and refrigerate 1 hour while preparing the filling.

Prepare the filling: Place a stainless steel bowl on top of a pot of boiling water, making a double boiler. In the bowl, melt the chocolate; then add the raisins, almonds, cardamom, and cinnamon. In a separate pan, melt the apricot glaze; then add to the chocolate mixture. Set aside to cool.

Preheat the oven to 350°.

Assemble the cookies: Remove the dough from the refrigerator. Roll into rectangles about 2 inches wide and 4 inches long. In the center of each rectangle, spoon the filling along the length; then roll the outer edge over the filling, enclosing the filling with the dough. Continue rolling the dough until the filling is completely enclosed. Brush egg wash along the seams and place the dough, seam down, on greased baking sheets.

With a sharp knife, make a slit at the center of each roll. Bake 20 minutes. When golden brown, remove from the oven and let cool. Before serving, dust with powdered sugar and slice through the roll at the slits that were started. Arrange on a platter with the macaroons.

CHRISTMAS DAY MENU

Potato-Leek Soup

White Bean, Raisin, and Almond Salad

*Roast Leg of Lamb in Natural Juices
    with Roasted Garlic and Ginger*

Sliced Potatoes in Chicken Stock with Onion and Thyme

Braised Shallots with Vinegar and Brown Sugar

Panettone

WHEN I THINK OF CHRISTMAS, I think of the mystery of life, how any newborn is a celebration, and how he or she may be a god. I believe we are all god-like and the newborn helps us see that.

We are given the gift of life and what we do with it is our gift to God. Am I only going to take from the group or am I going to give back, helping other people live a richer life? Only through love and service can I find happiness.

When I think of the epiphany, when the wise men were receptive and open to the thought that a child was the son of God, I think of the program, and being open to a new way. I examined my conscience, admitted my wrongs, and tried to change, always remembering I am only human and cannot do it alone. I believe every day in recovery is Christmas; it is only by grace that I found this program. The church could never save me from myself, but the program could.

Potato-Leek Soup

6 servings

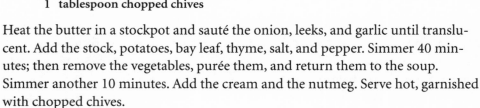

1 tablespoon butter
1 onion, thinly sliced
4 leek stalks (white part only), sliced
2 garlic cloves, thinly sliced
2 quarts chicken or vegetable stock
6 potatoes, peeled and diced
1 bay leaf
2 sprigs fresh thyme or 2 teaspoons dry thyme
2 teaspoons salt
1 teaspoon black pepper
½ teaspoon nutmeg
1 cup heavy cream
1 tablespoon chopped chives

Heat the butter in a stockpot and sauté the onion, leeks, and garlic until translucent. Add the stock, potatoes, bay leaf, thyme, salt, and pepper. Simmer 40 minutes; then remove the vegetables, purée them, and return them to the soup. Simmer another 10 minutes. Add the cream and the nutmeg. Serve hot, garnished with chopped chives.

White Bean, Raisin, and Almond Salad

6 servings

This is a very eye-catching salad with an array of colors and textures that blend together in a natural way.

1 head radicchio
3 cups cooked white beans
1 cup raisins, soaked 20 minutes in hot water
1 cup sliced roasted almonds
4 tablespoons virgin olive oil

2 tablespoons balsamic vinegar
1 tablespoon sun-dried tomatoes, sliced and rehydrated in hot water
2 tablespoons grated carrots

Core the head of radicchio and peel off the leaves to form a natural cup. In a mixing bowl, combine the white beans, raisins, almonds, olive oil, balsamic vinegar, and sun-dried tomatoes. Place the radicchio leaves on a plate, place a cup of salad in the center, and garnish with carrots.

THE FOLLOWING THREE RECIPES make up the main course in the Christmas Day menu.

Roast Leg of Lamb in Natural Juices with Roasted Garlic and Ginger

6 servings

5 pounds leg of lamb, boned and tied (ask your butcher to include the bones, which are for the sauce)

MARINADE
2 tablespoons virgin olive oil
4 garlic cloves, thinly sliced
4 sprigs rosemary
  juice of 1 lemon

SAUCE
1 tablespoon tomato paste
1 head garlic
1 teaspoon virgin olive oil
1 quart brown beef stock
1 cup cider vinegar
1 cup soy sauce
1 cup grated ginger (see note)
1 bay leaf
2 tablespoons cornstarch

Prepare the marinade: Combine the olive oil, garlic, rosemary, and lemon. Rub on the leg of lamb and let marinate 2 hours.

Preheat the oven to 350°.

Cook the lamb: Place the leg of lamb and the bones on a roasting rack in a large roasting pan. Roast about 1 hour. Use a meat thermometer to check the internal temperature of the lamb; it will be 130° when done. Remove the meat from the roasting pan and let it rest 1 hour before it is sliced.

Prepare the sauce: In the meantime, rub the bones with the tomato paste and return them to the roasting pan. Roast the bones another 1 hour. After about 40 minutes, rub the head of garlic with the olive oil. Place in a small baking dish and roast until soft (about 30 minutes). When finished, let cool, remove from the skin, and purée.

Remove the roasting pan from the oven and place it on top of the stove. Add the beef stock to the roasting pan and deglaze over medium heat, scraping the brown bits from the bottom of the pan. Add the vinegar, soy sauce, ginger, and bay leaf and simmer for 1 hour. The aroma of the lamb, tomato paste, and ginger will fill your home and rev up your appetite before you taste one bite of food.

Preheat the oven to 400°.

Strain the stock and thicken with cornstarch dissolved in 2 tablespoons cold water. Season with puréed garlic.

When ready to serve, return the roast to the oven and heat 20 minutes. Slice and cover with the lamb juice.

NOTE: Ginger helps thin the blood and lower blood cholesterol. It also helps prevent nausea. You can take a teaspoon of ginger powder in a capsule or 1 tablespoon of grated ginger in a cup of hot water as a tea to help with motion sickness.

Sliced Potatoes in Chicken Stock with Onion and Thyme

6 servings

8 russet potatoes, peeled and sliced ¼ inch thick
1 onion, thinly sliced
1 bay leaf
2 sprigs fresh thyme (or 1 teaspoon dried thyme)
2 teaspoons salt
1 teaspoon black pepper
1 quart chicken stock

Preheat the oven to 350°. Overlap the potato slices on the bottom of a large roasting pan. Spread the onion over the top. Add the bay leaf, thyme, salt, pepper, and chicken stock. Place on the stove and bring to a boil; then put into the oven and bake 40 minutes, or until the potatoes are tender.

Braised Shallots with Vinegar and Brown Sugar

6 servings

1 teaspoon virgin olive oil
4 cups shallots, peeled and left whole
2 tablespoons brown sugar
1 cup cider vinegar
1 cup chicken stock
½ cup soy sauce

Preheat the oven to 400°. Heat the olive oil in a large ovenproof sauté pan and sauté the shallots. Add the brown sugar and caramelize 3 to 4 minutes. Deglaze with the vinegar and reduce the liquid by half. Add the stock and soy sauce and bring to a boil. Bake 20 minutes or until the shallots are tender.

MAIN COURSE ASSEMBLY: Place the sliced lamb along the bottom of the serving platter, the potatoes at 2 o'clock, and the shallots at 11 o'clock and cover the lamb with the lamb juice.

Panettone

Makes 2 cakes

In Italy, panettone is the traditional Christmastime sweet bread. Developed in Milan, this fragrant yeast bread is studded with fruit and nuts and flavored with citrus. Leftover panettone makes a wonderful substitute for bread in French toast or bread pudding recipes.

⅔ cup lukewarm water
1 tablespoon (1 envelope) dry yeast
1 cup bread flour
1 teaspoon grated orange peel
1 cup butter
1 teaspoon grated lemon peel
2 teaspoons vanilla extract
1 teaspoon almond extract
6 eggs
1 cup orange juice
1 cup raisins
1 cup golden raisins
1 cup sliced almonds
5 cups all-purpose flour

In the bowl of a stand mixer, combine the water, yeast, and bread flour and let ferment 30 minutes to form a sponge.

In a large bowl, mix the orange peel, butter, lemon peel, vanilla and almond extracts, eggs, and orange juice. Add to the sponge and let ferment 10 minutes.

Add the raisins, golden raisins, and almonds to the sponge. Gradually add the all-purpose flour and mix 10 minutes with a dough hook at low speed, dusting as you go with flour, so the dough does not stick to the sides of the bowl. Place the dough in a large bowl, cover with plastic wrap, and let proof (rise) until double in size, about 1 hour.

Turn the dough out onto a floured work area. Knead for a couple of minutes and then divide the dough in half. Roll the dough into two 10-inch logs and place into 2 greased charlotte molds or other tall round baking pans. Let rise 1 hour until almost double in size.

Preheat the oven to 400°. Slit the tops of the logs with a sharp knife and bake 10 minutes. Lower the oven heat to 350° and bake another 30 minutes until golden. Remove from the oven and let cool 10 minutes. Unmold the bread and place on a rack to finish cooling. When cooled, brush with glaze.

GLAZE
- ½ cup water
- ½ cup butter (1 stick)
- 1 cup apricot glaze
- 1 cup powdered sugar

In a saucepan, place all the ingredients and melt slowly on the stove over low heat. Brush onto the bread.

NEW YEAR'S EVE BUFFET

Vegetable Soup

Grilled Salmon on a Bed of Pinto Beans and Feta Cheese

Pan-seared Chicken with Tortelloni and Chipotle Peppers

Bulgur Wheat with Roasted Parsnips, Turnips, Carrots, and Onion

Chocolate-dipped Strawberries

Chocolate Truffles

NEW YEAR'S EVE, with its traditional emphasis on champagne and parties, can be intimidating to someone new to recovery. Dancing and fellowship in a supportive recovery environment makes the holiday less threatening. The first time I danced in recovery—which may have been the first time I danced sober—I felt so awkward. But now that time has passed and I've danced on many a New Year's Eve, I feel more comfortable and more connected to my body. I feel like I'm Jackie Gleason out there on the dance floor.

At Hazelden New York we have a New Year's Eve dance for the residents and alumni. Surrounded by friends and loved ones, we celebrate the past year and the gifts our recovery has brought us. I prepare a buffet and decorate the hall to create a festive feeling. Hearty winter dishes with roasted vegetables and steaming soup keep us warm on the inside and remind us of the warmth of the fellowship as we approach the new year not with our old desperation and isolation, but with hope and meaning.

Vegetable Soup

6 servings

 1 tablespoon virgin olive oil
 1 onion, sliced
 2 garlic cloves, minced
 1 turnip, peeled and diced
 2 parsnips, peeled and diced
 4 carrots, peeled and diced
 2 leeks (white part only), sliced
 2 celery stalks, diced
 ½ cup tomato paste
 1 cup crushed tomatoes
 5 potatoes, peeled and diced
 1 cup yucca, diced (see note)
 3 quarts vegetable stock or water
 2 teaspoons salt
 1 teaspoon pepper
 1 bay leaf
 1 teaspoon chili powder
 ½ teaspoon cumin
 1 cup chopped cilantro
 2 jalapeño peppers, diced (use latex gloves or your hands will burn)
   juice of 1 lemon
   cilantro sprigs

Heat the olive oil in a large stockpot and sauté the onion and garlic until translucent. Add the turnip, parsnips, and carrots and continue cooking over medium heat, stirring occasionally. When the vegetables begin to caramelize, add the leeks and celery and continue to cook 4 to 6 minutes. Add the tomato paste and stir. Continue to cook over medium heat, allowing the paste and vegetables to become a deep brown, but be careful not to let them burn. Add the crushed tomatoes, potatoes, yucca, and stock. Bring to a boil. Add the salt, pepper, bay leaf, chili powder, and cumin, and simmer 40 minutes, or until the potatoes and yucca are tender. Add the jalapeño and cilantro and simmer another 10 minutes. The soup will become thick from the natural vegetable starches. When ready to serve, add the lemon juice and garnish with a sprig of cilantro.

NOTE: Yucca is a root vegetable used in Spanish cooking to thicken soups and stews. The peel is smooth and waxy; the flesh is firm and crisp. It is a single root (like a carrot), brought to the market in winter.

Grilled Salmon
on a Bed of Pinto Beans and Feta Cheese

6 servings

12 2-ounce pieces of salmon fillet

MARINADE
1 tablespoon virgin olive oil
 juice of 1 lemon
1 teaspoon chopped dill
2 garlic cloves, thinly sliced
2 teaspoons salt
1 teaspoon black pepper

PINTO BEANS
1 cup dried pinto beans (soaked overnight)
1 bay leaf
2 teaspoons salt
1 teaspoon black pepper

DRESSING
6 tablespoons virgin olive oil
2 tablespoons cider vinegar
 juice of 1 lemon
1 teaspoon hot sauce
2 teaspoons salt
1 red onion, thinly sliced

1 cup chopped fresh dill (or 2 teaspoons dried dill)

3 cups feta cheese, broken into pieces

1 cup black olives

1 cup green olives

  fresh dill sprigs

Prepare the marinade: Blend the olive oil, lemon juice, dill, garlic, salt, and pepper in a small bowl. Rub the mixture on the salmon pieces and marinate 2 hours.

Prepare the beans: Drain the soaked pinto beans. Place in a stockpot with 1 gallon of water, the bay leaf, salt, and pepper. Cook until the beans are tender, about 1 hour. Drain, remove the bay leaf, and cool the beans to room temperature.

Prepare the dressing: Combine the olive oil, vinegar, lemon juice, hot sauce, and salt in a large mixing bowl. Toss with the onion, dill, feta, olives, and cooked pinto beans. Let marinate 2 hours.

Cook the salmon: Grill the salmon 3 minutes on each side. Arrange the beans on a large platter, place the salmon on top of the beans, and garnish with sprigs of fresh dill.

Pan-seared Chicken with Tortelloni and Chipotle Peppers

6 servings

6 boneless chicken breast halves, trimmed of fat and skin

MARINADE

2 tablespoons virgin olive oil

  juice of 1 lemon

2 teaspoons salt

1 teaspoon black pepper

1 tablespoon chopped chipotle peppers (see note)

TORTELLONI

1 gallon water

1 teaspoon salt

1 teaspoon virgin olive oil
1 pound tortelloni

SAUCE
2 tablespoons balsamic vinegar
  juice of 1 lemon
6 tablespoons virgin olive oil
1 red pepper, diced
1 yellow pepper, diced
1 cup sun-dried tomatoes rehydrated in hot water
1 red onion, diced
1 teaspoon salt
1 teaspoon black pepper
1 teaspoon hot sauce
1 teaspoon cumin
1 tablespoon chopped fresh cilantro
  fresh cilantro and slices of lemon for garnish

Prepare the marinade: Blend the olive oil, lemon juice, salt, pepper, and chipotle peppers. Rub on the chicken breasts and let marinate 2 hours.

Prepare the tortelloni: In a large stockpot, bring the water, salt, and olive oil to a rapid boil. Add the tortelloni and cook 6 to 8 minutes until tender to your liking. (I will not tell you to cook the pasta al dente. You cook it the way you prefer; after all, you are the one eating it!)

When the tortelloni is done, drain and run cold water over it to stop the cooking process. Place in a bowl and cover with plastic wrap.

Prepare the sauce: Whisk together the balsamic vinegar, lemon juice, and olive oil. Combine with the diced peppers, sun-dried tomatoes, diced onion, salt, pepper, hot sauce, cumin, and cilantro. Toss the mixture with the tortelloni and marinate 2 hours.

Cook the chicken: In a large sauté pan, brown the chicken breasts about 6 minutes on each side. (You may need to use 2 pans or sauté the breasts in batches.) Place the sautéed chicken on a cutting board and slice across the breast, cutting into 2-inch strips. Add to the tortelloni and toss. Mound on a platter and garnish with sprigs of fresh cilantro and slices of lemon. The mound of pasta gives the appearance of abundance. No one likes to take food from a platter that looks empty.

NOTE: Chipotles are smoked jalapeño peppers. They add heat and a smoky flavor to any dish and are great in barbecue sauces. You can purchase them dried or canned. Wear plastic gloves while handling these peppers.

Bulgur Wheat with Roasted Parsnips, Turnips, Carrots, and Onion

6 servings

6 cups water
pinch of salt
3 cups bulgur wheat (see note)
2 tablespoons virgin olive oil
2 garlic cloves, sliced
2 teaspoons salt
1 teaspoon black pepper
2 teaspoons sugar
2 carrots, peeled and diced
2 turnips, peeled and diced
2 parsnips, peeled and diced
1 red onion, sliced

DRESSING
6 tablespoons virgin olive oil
2 tablespoons cider vinegar
juice of 1 lemon
1 teaspoon salt
½ teaspoon black pepper
1 tablespoon chopped Italian parsley
2 sprigs fresh thyme

Prepare the bulgar wheat: Bring the water to a boil, add salt and the bulgur wheat, and cook 20 to 25 minutes. When the bulgur is done (tender but not soft), drain and rinse under cold water in a strainer. Place in a large bowl and cover with plastic wrap.

Prepare the vegetables: Preheat the oven to 350°. Blend the olive oil, garlic, salt, pepper, and sugar. Toss with the diced carrots, turnips, parsnips, and onion to coat evenly. Place the vegetables on a baking sheet and roast until they are tender and begin to caramelize. The dry heat of the oven brings out the natural sweetness of the vegetables and maintains their crispness. When the vegetables are done, add them to the bulgur wheat.

Prepare the dressing: Blend the ingredients and combine with the bulgur and vegetables. Place in a decorative bowl and garnish with Italian parsley.

NOTE: Bulgur wheat is similar to cracked wheat but cooks much faster. Bulgur consists of the parched, steamed, then dried wheatberries. It has a mild taste and crunchy texture when cooked correctly. It is frequently used in the Middle East and can be purchased in health food stores and well-stocked supermarkets.

Chocolate-dipped Strawberries

6 servings

This is a very simple yet elegant dessert. When you bite into the strawberry, you will first experience the crisp chocolate and then the strawberry's soft, moist texture. Use the best quality chocolate you can find for the best results.

2 pints fresh strawberries
1 pound semisweet chocolate
1 tablespoon canola oil

Leave the stems on the strawberries, rinse with water, place on absorbent paper, and pat dry.

Place the chocolate in a glass or stainless steel bowl, making sure the bowl is dry. (There is nothing worse for chocolate than water.) Place the bowl of chocolate over a pan half-filled with boiling water. When the chocolate is melted, add the oil and remove from heat. Add in a little piece of unmelted chocolate; this brings down the temperature and gives the chocolate a nice shine.

Place the strawberries on wooden skewers stem side down and dip the head of the strawberry into the chocolate. Transfer to parchment paper and refrigerate. When you are ready to serve, place the strawberries on a serving platter lined with a doily.

Chocolate Truffles

Makes 24 truffles

> 1 pound semisweet chocolate, chopped
> 2 cups heavy cream
>   powdered sugar
> 1 cup cocoa powder

Combine the chopped chocolate and heavy cream in a dry glass or stainless steel bowl. Place the bowl over a pot half-filled with boiling water, letting the steam melt the chocolate. When the chocolate is melted, pour into a shallow pan and refrigerate at least 2 hours.

When the chocolate is solid enough to mold, remove from the refrigerator. With a spoon, scrape off enough chocolate to make a 1-inch truffle. Dust your hands with powdered sugar and roll the chocolate into a ball. Repeat until you have used all the chocolate. Refrigerate the truffles for 1 hour; then roll in cocoa powder, covering the truffle completely. The bitter cocoa contrasts nicely with the sweet chocolate and the creamy texture.

NEW YEAR'S DAY BRUNCH

Hoppin' John Soup

Julienne of Endive and Fennel with Arugula and Orange Wedges

Onion-Mushroom Quiche with Wild Rice Crust

Glazed Carrots, Turnips, and Apples

White Chocolate Mousse in Tulip Cups

ONE OF THE GREAT PLEASURES I have at Hazelden New York is watching the alumni come back during the holiday season. You can see the dramatic transformation from scared and angry residents to confident alumni. It's wonderful to watch them making plans for the future, enjoying life, opening businesses, getting married and having children, beginning life all over again. The miracle is right there, reminding me why I am here at Hazelden. When residents first come to us it is so hard for them to be part of the community, always finding reasons to eat alone and not join in. And now I get to watch them stand around a holiday buffet table, chatting and enjoying life.

Hoppin' John Soup

6 servings

This typical southern soup is traditionally served on New Year's Day. It is supposed to bring good luck. As the custom goes, the cook puts a penny in the pot when the soup has finished cooking, and the person who has the bowl of soup with the penny in it will have good fortune for the coming year.

4 ounces andouille sausage, sliced ¼ inch thick
1 onion, chopped
2 garlic cloves, thinly sliced
2 turnips, peeled and diced
2 carrots
2 quarts chicken stock
1 teaspoon salt
½ teaspoon black pepper
2 cups black-eyed peas soaked overnight
1 cup cooked rice
8 cups mustard greens (about 1 large bunch), cleaned and trimmed
1 teaspoon chili oil (see page 84)

In a large heavy stockpot, brown the sausage; then pour off excess fat. Add the onion and garlic and continue cooking until translucent. Add the turnips and carrots and continue cooking 6 to 8 minutes, stirring occasionally. Add the stock, salt, pepper, and black-eyed peas, and simmer 1 hour. Add the rice and mustard greens and simmer another 20 minutes. When ready to serve, drizzle chili oil over the top.

Julienne of Endive and Fennel with Arugula and Orange Wedges

6 servings

- 2 endives
- 2 fennel bulbs
- 4 oranges
- 2 bunches arugula, washed and stemmed

DRESSING
- 3 tablespoons virgin olive oil
- 1 tablespoon balsamic vinegar
- juice of ½ lemon
- 1 teaspoon salt
- ½ teaspoon black pepper

Cut the endives and fennel bulbs in half lengthwise, core, and cut into strips lengthwise, about ⅛ inch wide.

Peel the oranges, removing the white membrane, and cut them into wedges, making beautiful, bright-orange sections free of all skin and membrane.

Prepare the dressing: Whisk together the olive oil, balsamic vinegar, lemon juice, salt, and pepper. In a large bowl, combine the endive, fennel, oranges, and arugula and toss gently with the dressing. To serve, mound on chilled plates.

THE FOLLOWING TWO RECIPES make up the main course in the New Year's Day brunch.

Onion-Mushroom Quiche with Wild Rice Crust

6 to 8 servings

WILD RICE CRUST

2 cups uncooked wild rice
6 cups water
1 teaspoon salt
½ teaspoon black pepper
1 bay leaf
1 clove
1 cup toasted sesame seeds
3 tablespoons tahini paste
1 cup whole wheat flour
4 teaspoons soy sauce

QUICHE

2 teaspoons olive oil
4 cups mushrooms, sliced
1½ teaspoons salt
1 onion, thinly sliced
1 quart heavy cream
4 eggs
4 egg yolks
½ teaspoon pepper
¼ teaspoon nutmeg
1 tablespoon all-purpose flour

Prepare the crust: In a stockpot, combine the wild rice, water, salt, pepper, bay leaf, and clove. Bring to a boil and simmer 40 minutes until the rice is soft. Drain and let cool.

In a large bowl, combine the rice with the toasted sesame seeds, tahini paste, whole wheat flour, and soy sauce.

Spray nonstick coating onto a tart pan with a removable bottom. Press the mixture into the tart pan, making a crust, lining the entire pan. Refrigerate 1 hour.

Prepare the quiche: Preheat the oven to 350°.

Heat 1 teaspoon olive oil and sauté the mushrooms, add ½ teaspoon salt and a pinch of pepper, and cook until tender. Cool, then disperse over the bottom of the wild rice crust.

Heat the remaining teaspoon of olive oil and sauté the onion until it begins to caramelize. Spread over the mushrooms.

Thoroughly blend the cream, eggs, egg yolks, 1 teaspoon salt, pepper, nutmeg, and flour. Pour the liquid through a fine-mesh sieve over the onion and mushrooms and bake 40 minutes or until the filling sets. Remove from the oven and let cool. When cooled, lift the bottom of the pan (with the quiche in it) up through the ring. Cut into wedges.

Glazed Carrots, Turnips, and Apples

6 servings

> 1   tablespoon olive oil
> 4   carrots, peeled and thinly sliced
> 4   turnips, peeled and thinly sliced
> 2   apples, cored, peeled, and thinly sliced
> 1   tablespoon sugar
> 1   teaspoon salt
> ½   teaspoon black pepper
> ¼   teaspoon cardamom
>   Italian (flat leaf) parsley sprig

In a sauté pan, heat the olive oil, and add the carrots and turnips. Sauté 6 to 8 minutes, stirring occasionally. When the vegetables begin to caramelize, add a few drops of water to create steam. Repeat this until the vegetables are tender but crisp. Add the apples, sugar, salt, pepper, and cardamom. Continue cooking until the sugar is dissolved and the apples are soft.

> MAIN COURSE ASSEMBLY: Place the quiche in the center with the carrots, turnips, and apples around it to make a frame. Garnish with a sprig of Italian parsley.

White Chocolate Mousse in Tulip Cups

6 servings

This will be the last thing you eat on New Year's Day and it will be a real bang!
It is a signature dessert your guests will always remember.

TULIP CUPS

1 cup sugar

1 cup ground almonds (buy sliced almonds and grind in a food processor;
consistency should be chunky, not powdery)

2 eggs

2 tablespoons all-purpose flour

WHITE CHOCOLATE MOUSSE

2 cups sugar

5 tablespoons water

1 teaspoon lemon juice

½ cup egg whites (about 3 egg whites)

1 pound white chocolate, cut into 1-inch pieces

2 cups heavy cream, whipped
raspberry purée, fresh strawberries, and mint for garnish

Prepare the tulip cups: Preheat the oven to 350°.

Blend the sugar, ground almonds, eggs, and flour in a mixing bowl.

Spray 2 sheet pans and 6 small bowls (about 3 inches in diameter) or custard
cups with nonstick pan coating. With a tablespoon, spoon the mixture in 6
dollops onto the pans, using the back of the spoon to spread each dollop into
a circle, about 6 inches in diameter. Bake until the edges are brown (about
5 minutes). Remove from the oven.

When still warm, remove the cookies from the pan with a dough scraper. Working
quickly before the cookies cool, place them in the small bowls and form the cookie
into the bowl, making a tulip shape. When completely cooled, remove from the
bowls and store in a cool, dry place.

Prepare the mousse: Wipe a mixing bowl with a little white vinegar on a paper
towel to remove any oils so that the egg whites will whip well. Rinse and towel dry.

Also do this with the wire whip or beater you will be using. When separating egg whites, be sure not to include any yolk, otherwise they will not peak.

Combine the sugar and water in a small saucepan and cook over medium heat until the mixture reaches 240° on a candy thermometer; this is called a "soft ball."

When the syrup is almost at the right temperature, start whipping the egg whites at a high speed. When the egg whites begin to peak, add the cooked syrup slowly in a thin stream while continually whipping the egg whites. This will make a meringue, thick and light. When no more steam is released from the meringue, add the white chocolate pieces. The heat from the meringue will melt the chocolate somewhat, leaving smaller chunks of chocolate. It is important not to overmix, so once you have added the chocolate, mix only long enough to disperse the chocolate evenly. When the meringue is at room temperature, fold in the whipped cream gently and refrigerate the meringue.

Line the bottoms of six dessert plates with raspberry purée. You can purchase the purée frozen. Thaw and use as an instant sauce. Place a tulip cup in the center of each plate, spoon the mousse into the cups, and garnish with sliced strawberries and a sprig of mint.

MARTIN LUTHER KING DAY MENU

Collard Greens with Smoked Chicken Breast
   and Onion in Chicken Broth

Barbecued Ribs

Braised Mustard Greens

Macaroni and Cheese

Vanilla Wafers in Vanilla Pudding
   Topped with Cocoa Powder and Powdered Sugar

EVERY TIME I HEAR MARTIN LUTHER KING'S 1963 SPEECH at the Civil Rights March in Washington, I get emotional. When he says, "I have a dream my four little children…will not be judged by the color of their skin, but by the content of their character," he is talking about putting principles before personalities, acknowledging that everyone has the right to reach his or her potential. And when a hand reaches out to us, it is our responsibility to reach back, no matter whose hand is reaching out to us.

The lesson of the pain and humiliation of discrimination was brought home to me when I was working in a restaurant. I was up for a promotion at the time and was surprised when the chef overlooked me. When I asked him why, he said my culinary skills and natural feel for the kitchen were not enough, that the staff would not follow me because of my weight. All I wanted was a chance to do the job that I knew I could do. It was a devastating experience that I never forgot.

I try to remember that lesson and honor King's legacy by preparing a special menu. I like to serve these dishes family style, with platters of ribs and serving bowls loaded with macaroni and cheese and sautéed greens. Passing the food around the table, serving from the same dishes, is an intimate experience and helps remind us that everyone has a place at the table.

Collard Greens with Smoked Chicken Breast and Onion in Chicken Broth

6 servings

1 teaspoon virgin olive oil
1 onion, thinly sliced
½ pound smoked chicken breast, sliced on an angle
3 bunches collard greens, washed and stemmed
½ teaspoon salt
¼ teaspoon black pepper
1 quart chicken stock, preferably homemade

Heat the olive oil in a stockpot and sauté the onion until it begins to caramelize, stirring occasionally. Add the smoked chicken breast and cook over medium heat for 5 minutes, releasing the wonderful smoky flavors. Add the collards and continue cooking until the leaves begin to wilt. Add the seasonings and stock and continue simmering until the greens are tender, about 12 minutes, and serve in a bowl.

Barbecued Ribs

6 servings

SAUCE

1 cup chili sauce
½ cup ketchup
½ cup tomato purée
1 tablespoon prepared yellow mustard
4 tablespoons honey
2 teaspoons hot sauce
1 cup apple cider
4 tablespoons chopped chipotle peppers
1 teaspoon salt
½ teaspoon black pepper
2 ounces espresso (ask your local coffee shop for a double espresso)

RIBS

4   pounds ribs (ask the butcher for 3-inch down ribs,
    or, if you prefer smaller ribs, ask for baby back ribs)

Prepare the sauce: Preheat the oven to 350°.

With a wire whisk, combine all the sauce ingredients in a mixing bowl. Adjust the seasonings to your liking, maybe a little sweeter or hotter.

Prepare the ribs: Place the ribs in the oven and roast 30 minutes on each side. Brush sauce on the ribs and roast another 15 minutes, turn and brush the other side with sauce, and roast 15 minutes again. Take from the oven, brush tops again with sauce, and serve.

Braised Mustard Greens

6 servings

½   cup almonds, sliced
2   ancho chili peppers
4   strips bacon, diced
½   onion, thinly sliced
2   garlic cloves, thinly sliced
1   tomato, diced
4   bunches mustard greens, stemmed and washed
2   tablespoons cider vinegar
½   cup chicken stock, preferably homemade
¼   teaspoon salt
⅛   teaspoon black pepper

Preheat the oven to 400°.

Toast the almonds on a sheet pan for 5 minutes.

Skewer the chilies and toast over the flame of a gas stove or the high heat of an electric stove about 1 minute; then dice and set aside. Be sure to wear gloves to avoid getting the chili oil on your skin.

In a skillet, cook the bacon over medium heat. When the bacon becomes brown, drain excess fat, add the onion and garlic, and continue cooking. Add the ancho chilies and tomato; then add the mustard greens and continue cooking until the leaves are wilted. Add the vinegar and stock. When the greens are tender, add the almonds, season to taste, and serve.

Macaroni and Cheese

6 servings

1 pound elbow macaroni

SAUCE

10 ounces grated mild cheddar cheese
1 quart milk
4 eggs
4 egg yolks
½ teaspoon salt
¼ teaspoon black pepper
1 teaspoon paprika
¼ teaspoon nutmeg

TOPPING

½ cup dry breadcrumbs
2 ounces grated cheddar cheese

Preheat the oven to 300°.

Prepare the macaroni: Bring a pot of salted water to boil. Add the macaroni and cook until tender. Drain in a colander and set aside.

Prepare the sauce: In a mixing bowl, combine the cheese, milk, eggs, egg yolks, salt, pepper, paprika, and nutmeg. Add the macaroni and stir until well blended. Place in a greased baking dish, cover, and bake 1 hour or until firm.

Prepare the topping: Mix together the breadcrumbs and 2 ounces grated cheddar cheese.

Remove the cover from the baking dish, top with the breadcrumb mixture, and increase the temperature to 350°. Bake 10 minutes until the top is brown. Serve hot.

Vanilla Wafers in Vanilla Pudding Topped with Cocoa Powder and Powdered Sugar

6 servings

NOTE: This dessert needs to be prepared a day in advance. I like to use a fresh vanilla bean in this recipe. Vanilla beans can be purchased in the spice section of grocery stores, at gourmet shops, or (most economically) at food co-ops. To store vanilla beans, place them in a container with granulated sugar. This keeps the beans fresh and gives the sugar a vanilla flavor. In my professional kitchen, I reuse a single bean two or three times.

8 cups cold milk
2 cups granulated sugar
1 vanilla bean, split (or 2 teaspoons vanilla extract)
1 cup cornstarch
4 whole eggs
8 egg yolks
½ cup soft butter
1 2-pound box vanilla wafers

TOPPING
½ cup cocoa powder
½ cup powdered sugar

In a saucepan, combine 7 cups of the milk, 1 cup of the granulated sugar, and the split vanilla bean. Begin to cook at medium heat.

In a mixing bowl, whisk the other 1 cup of milk with the cornstarch, dissolving completely, making sure there are no lumps. Whisk in the eggs, yolks, and remaining cup of the granulated sugar. Set aside.

When the pot of milk comes to a boil, remove the vanilla bean and, with a paring knife, scrape the tiny black seeds inside the bean into the hot milk. You will see little black specks in the milk, which lets people know you have used fresh vanilla. No matter how high the quality of vanilla extract, it cannot compare with that of a fresh vanilla bean.

Remove the mixture from the stove and whisk 1 cup into the egg mixture, whisking constantly. Repeat this process, 1 cup of hot milk at a time, until all the milk is added to the egg mixture. By adding the hot milk slowly, you temper the mixture so the eggs do not curdle.

Place the mixture back into the saucepan and bring to a boil. Within a couple of minutes, it should become thick and creamy. Stir in the soft butter, giving the cream a nice shine.

Line an oiled baking dish with some of the vanilla wafers. Pour the pudding into the dish of wafers, spread evenly, and line the top with another row of vanilla wafers.

Prepare the topping: Combine the cocoa powder and powdered sugar. Dust the entire top of the cookies heavily with the mixture. Place in the refrigerator and let sit overnight.

When ready to serve, scoop the dessert into individual dishes, making sure each scoop contains 1 wafer.

THOUGHTS ON RECOVERY

My sponsor always tells me, "God moves mountains, but we have to bring the shovels." For so much of my life, I felt that the "good" things were not for me and that nothing I could do would change that. In recovery, however, I discovered that is not true. I no longer believe that God chooses, that this one has good and that one does not. If I really want something, I can work for it. Setting standards and meeting them takes self-discipline, which is the key to any success. Making healthy choices about what to do with my life is the foundation of my spiritual condition. Not trying to understand but accepting that this is the way it is. All I have is *today* and what I do with it.

Barbara Sanders hurries off to serve individual pizzas fresh from the oven.

The facade of Hazelden New York

Glossary

Ancho chile Dried poblano chile peppers, usually dark red in color, rich, and somewhat sweet in flavor.

Basmati rice An aromatic white long-grained rice with a natural nutty flavor.

Black bean paste A flavoring agent in Chinese cooking made of fermented black beans. It has a salty, meaty taste. You can purchase it in most gourmet and Asian specialty stores.

Braise A cooking technique in which the food, usually meat, is browned at a high heat, then is slowly cooked tightly covered, with liquid slowly at low heat, either in the oven or on the stove. The food becomes very tender and flavorful.

Brazier A heavy-gauge pan designed specifically for braising. It has a handle on each side and a tight-fitting lid. Braziers come in many shapes, most commonly round, square, and rectangle.

Broth A clear liquid made by simmering both meat and bones in water. Broth can be served alone, as opposed to a stock, which serves as a base for other preparations. Broth has a more robust flavor than stock because the base of the liquid is from meat and bones rather than bones alone. To ensure clarity, it is essential to regulate the temperature of the broth as it cooks, never letting the liquid rise above a slow simmer and skimming the surface to remove impurities.

Bulgur wheat A parched cracked wheat that is a staple in North African cooking. It makes delicious salads such as tabbouleh.

Caramelize To extract and brown the natural sugars from an ingredient (usually vegetables) through heat, usually by sautéing or roasting, turning the food a delicious golden brown and intensifying the sweetness. Sugar is often caramelized in baked goods and other desserts, such as crème caramel.

Chipotle peppers Dried and smoked jalepeño peppers, chipotles are very rich, smooth, smoky, and sweet in flavor. They are available dried or canned.

Couscous Very small wheat pasta. A staple of North African cooking, couscous is traditionally cooked with fragrant herbs, vegetables, and stock, and is often studded with nuts or tender chunks of meat.

Deglaze To lift the caramelized browned bits of food from the bottom of the pan after roasting or sautéing. To

241

deglaze, add a small amount of liquid to the hot pan, gently scraping a wooden spoon against the bottom of the pan.

Dough cutter A spatula-like tool made specifically to cut dough.

Durum wheat A hard wheat that is high in gluten and often ground into semolina for making pasta.

Egg wash An egg slightly beaten with a small amount of water. It is used to seal the seams of pastries and pasta (ravioli) and is brushed on pastries and breads to create a glossy finish.

Farfel In Jewish cooking, farfel refers to food, often noodles or matzo, that is broken into small pieces.

Fermentation A chemical reaction of the breakdown of organic compounds produced by microorganisms or (most commonly) yeast. In baking, fermentation creates gas bubbles which cause dough to rise.

Floret The flowers of broccoli or cauliflower which are at the top of the stems.

French knife Also known as a chef's knife. An all purpose knife with a wide blade and straight back, with a heel and a tip. It is usually 10″ to 14″ in length. It is frequently used to cut vegetables.

Gluten A protein found in wheat and other grains. When flour is moistened and mixed, the gluten in the flour helps the dough hold it's shape, giving breads and other baked goods their elasticity.

Gratin A casserole or other dish topped with cheese or bread crumbs and heated until brown and crispy (for example, potatoes au gratin).

Grilling basket A cagelike tool used to place fragile or small foods on top of a grill so they do not stick or fall through to be lost to the ashy coals.

Hoisin A Chinese sauce, thick and brown in color. Sweet and slightly pungent, this mixture of garlic, soybeans, chili peppers, and spices is used in a multitude of Asian recipes.

Jicama A tan-skinned tuberous vegetable grown mainly in Mexico. Crisp and sweet, the white flesh makes a wonderful addition to a raw vegetable platter or in salads.

Julienne To cut food, especially vegetables, into very thin strips , like matchsticks.

Kugel A savory baked pudding served as a side dish for a Jewish Sabbath dinner.

Panettone A yeasted sweet bread, usually studded with fruit and nuts and flavored with citrus, that is a traditional Christmastime favorite in Italy.

Parmigiano-Reggiano cheese The premier parmesan cheese. A hard, sharp Italian cheese with a nutty, elegant flavor. It is part skim and part whole cow's milk. Aged for at least 18 months, this 700-year-old specialty from the Emilio-Romagna region of Italy needs a government stamp to be labeled authentic. Grate this cheese over pasta or soups. Parmigiano-Reggiano also makes an exciting addition to any cheese board. Stored in small pieces in air-tight containers in the refrigerator, it will keep up to 2 months.

Pecorino cheese Cheese made from sheep's milk. Pecorino Romano is a hard, sharp Italian cheese aged for at least one year. Stronger in flavor than Parmigiano-Reggiano, it is usually only used as a grating cheese. Store as you would Parmigiano-Reggiano.

Proof To let dough rise through the fermentation process. Carbon dioxide is released and then trapped in the gluten of the dough. Expanding air pockets cause the dough to rise, giving the bread texture and taste.

Purée A process by which whole foods are turned into a paste. There are many ways to puree foods, such as using a food processor or mashing through a strainer.

Quarry tile An unglazed clay tile that you can place in the oven to bake breads or pizzas with a crisp crust. Purchase in a tile store, but be sure it is unglazed.

Reduce To concentrate a liquid such as broth or stock by boiling it or sim-mering for extended periods of time. The evaporation of the liquid leaves a sauce that is thick and flavorful.

Render To extract fat from meats, such as bacon. The meat is heated slowly so that the fat melts and liquefies. When the meat becomes crisp or brown, it is removed from the heat and the fat is discarded.

Roux A mixture of melted butter and flour cooked over low heat and used to thicken sauces and soups. Roux is cooked to different degrees—white, blond, and brown—depending on the color and richness desired for your sauce. When using it to thicken soups or sauces, make sure you allow time to cook out the flour taste (this is deter-mined by taste).

Sauté To fry quickly in a skillet or sauté pan, using a small amount of fat.

Semolina A coarsely ground durum wheat used in making pastas and gnocchi.

Simmer To cook food gently in liquid at a temperature of about 180 degrees so the bubbles are tiny and just break-ing the surface. It is usually used to re-duce a liquid's volume while keeping it clear.

Sponge A bread-dough mixture con-sisting of water, yeast, and flour. The dough mixture is set aside and covered during the fermentation process until it bubbles and becomes foamy, resembling a sponge.

Stew A cooking method in which food is browned, then covered with liquid and simmered slowly over a period of time. Stewing tenderizes the ingredients, which is why tougher cuts of meat are often prepared this way.

Stock A strained liquid made from simmering bones, vegetables, and aromatics in water. Stock is used as a base for making soups and sauces. It is simmered over long periods of time, giving it a distinct flavor.

Sweat To cook vegetables in a small amount of fat, covered, over low heat until they are soft and translucent from cooking in their own juices.

Tube pan A round pan with deep sides and a hollow center tube used for baking ring cakes such as angel food and chiffon cakes. The tube promotes even baking of delicate batters. Some tube pans have removable sides.

Index

GINO DALESANDRO is currently the head chef at Hazelden New York. Trained at the Culinary Institute of America, Dalesandro has worked at numerous premier restaurants, including Sophie, Metropolis, Water Club, Helmsley Palace, and the Rainbow Room.